SPSS step by step

Essentials for social and political science

SPSS step by step

Essentials for social and political science

Cole Davis

First published in Great Britain in 2013 by

The Policy Press
University of Bristol
Fourth Floor
Beacon House
Queen's Road
Bristol BS8 1QU
UK
Tel +44 (0)117 331 4054
Fax +44 (0)117 331 4093
e-mail tpp-info@bristol.ac.uk
www.policypress.co.uk

North American office:
The Policy Press
c/o The University of Chicago Press
1427 East 60th Street
Chicago, IL 60637, USA
t: +1 773 702 7700
f: +1 773-702-9756
e:sales@press.uchicago.edu
www.press.uchicago.edu

© The Policy Press 2013

British Library Cataloguing in Publication Data
A catalogue record for this book is available
from the British Library.

Library of Congress Cataloging-in-Publication
Data
A catalog record for this book has been
requested.

ISBN 978 1 44730 627 6 paperback
ISBN 978 1 44730 628 3 hardcover

The statements and opinions contained within
this publication are solely those of the editors
and contributors and not of The University of
Bristol or The Policy Press. The University
of Bristol and The Policy Press disclaim
responsibility for any injury to persons or
property resulting from any material published
in this publication.

The Policy Press works to counter
discrimination on grounds of gender, race,
disability, age and sexuality.

Cover design by Qube Design Associates,
Bristol
Front cover: image kindly supplied by istock
Printed and bound in Great Britain by Hobbs,
Southampton
The Policy Press uses environmentally
responsible print partners

To the memory of my mother, Irene Deborah Davis

Contents

Part One
Background knowledge

Chapter 1
Introduction

Why this book was written

As an applied researcher, I was once asked to produce a training course on computerised statistics for researchers who did not understand or feel comfortable with statistics. I then found similar needs among the ranks of business people, accountants, the medical profession, civil servants, local government officials and last but certainly not least, students struggling with their research projects.

I looked for books which could ameliorate this situation and found that many were full of equations, satisfying a statistician's concern with mathematical rigour but repelling the ordinary reader. Others told you more than you needed to know as a beginner, so there was no way of knowing what was important and what was peripheral. The few better books either failed to address the data analysis requirements of the real world – primarily dealing with experimental situations – or told the user how to calculate the statistics by hand.

This is intended to be a highly practical book, designed to offer the reader a quick and easy introduction to the analysis of data. Fundamental concepts are presented in the first part of the book – which should be read for a proper understanding of statistical testing – but other ideas are introduced where they logically arise. Each statistical test is accompanied by a worked example, pertaining to social and political research or practical problems in business and other settings.

SPSS is incredibly rich in features. The SPSS manuals (IBM, 2011) and internet searches will provide more in-depth coverage of specific techniques, but this book is selective in its use of statistical procedures to stop you losing your way.

Similarly, although this book does make reference to research design, its primary focus is on statistical testing. There are plentiful sources of information on research design (for example, Davies, 2007; Creswell, 2008). Again, for the purposes of clarity, this book restricts its coverage to that which is clearly necessary.

Who is this book for?

The primary audience is obviously those needing to interpret and analyse data, both at beginner and intermediate level.

The reader may be undertaking research for the first time – within undergraduate research modules, part of a postgraduate project or undertaking a research project at work – or returning to research after a break.

As well as students and academic researchers, readers may be involved in applied research, conducting interviews, focus groups and survey questionnaires. Marketers, social and educational researchers, for example, may want to quantify the findings from their questionnaires. You can even turn information from interviews into quantifiable data by categorising it; the analysis of such information is covered in the chapter on qualitative research (Chapter 8).

Other readers such as business personnel may wish to add to their own market value by acquiring additional skills. As will be seen, this may include ascertaining whether or not a trend can be said to be significant. It may also involve working out which factors have the most influence on business outcomes. The chapter on survival analysis, rarely found in introductory books on statistics, will be of immediate interest to clinicians, although – in its other guise as 'the time until events' – it will be shown to be useful in a range of different settings.

People wanting to 'break into' data analysis may do well to start here.

What is new in this book?

Most introductory books in statistics merely offer a section on 'Chi Square'. Here, the whole of Chapter 8 is devoted to qualitative (or categorical) analysis.

Not all introductory books discuss multiple regression, a technique used more and more frequently in applied research.

New within an introductory book is survival analysis, the study of the time until events. This has been given many names and is, therefore, seen as a specialised technique in diverse fields, a peculiar paradox. In this book, I show that this set of techniques can be applied very widely indeed.

Apart from a tendency to champion the use of non-parametric tests in the study of everyday problems, my other innovations are mere literary tweaks.

The presentation of concepts in this book

Coherence, rather than comprehensiveness, is the key to this book. As an applied researcher, I do not feel constrained by the requirements of academic boards, so I will avoid squiggles and citations of formulae. (Ok, I do use numbers and decimals; into all gardens some rain must fall.)

I do not think it practical, however, to protect the reader from all statistical jargon. This will be met with when using any piece of statistical software, let alone when reading the reports of others, and any other books on statistics. Where appropriate, I introduce alternative names for various concepts as these will be found in different settings.

Each chapter ends with a 'controversy' section, or **talking point.** This tends to raise issues where the received wisdom may be erroneous or impractical.

There are also somewhat more in-depth discussions of statistical theory in 'ignore if you like' boxes. As with the rest of the book, these tend to avoid actual mathematics.

The part of the book offering background knowledge should be read in its entirety in order to make full sense of the practical work to come. As statistical testing is primarily about inferential statistics, my introduction to descriptive statistics is speedy and highly selective. But it does have a bearing on the preliminary analysis of data, which should be carried out before running tests, and it also offers a quick and basic guide to using SPSS.

That part of the book dealing with the analysis of differences is fairly conventional, apart from a slight leaning towards non-parametrics as more useful tools for data analysis 'in the field'.

The chapter on qualitative (or categorical) analysis offers a broader set of practical usages than is usually the case in more academic texts.

The chapter on relationships between data – correlations, regression and factor analysis – goes beyond some introductory texts in introducing both multiple regression and factor analysis. This reflects the increasing usage of multiple regression which, as will become obvious from the business exercise, has clear practical uses. With regards to factor analysis, it is often the sorry fate of people faced with doctoral projects (among others) to find themselves face-to-face with a problem requiring this and to discover that 'simple introductions' to factor analysis tend to be anything but simple. I hope that the minimalist treatment given here will meet the need for immediate action and will make it easier to absorb more in-depth texts because you will already have acquired a grasp of the essentials.

There is also coverage of factorial analysis of variance (for example, two-way ANOVA) and to some extent analysis of covariance (ANCOVA).

After covering the analysis of the time until events, traditionally used in health research as 'survival analysis' but with many other uses, the book culminates with a section which includes a short set of exercises. Unlike academic tests, exercises do not accompany each chapter: as practical research is not accompanied by a guide saying 'this problem is one which involves a t test'. It makes more sense to use your overall knowledge from the book to tackle these problems once you have read it through.

The chapter on the presentation of statistics for non-academic purposes is designed to satisfy organisations with practical concerns; readers with academic needs can use this book as a speedy way of gaining a fundamental understanding of statistics, but will need to move to more specific works of reference before writing academic reports. A brief discussion of some other types of statistical tests then follows.

Some data sets used for worked examples will be reused and built up as the book goes on in order to avoid the need for lengthy data entry. On the whole, small data sets have been chosen. Throughout the book, worked examples accompany the tests, with themes which should be of interest to various audiences. Unless explicitly stated otherwise, all data sets are fictional and should not be considered as supportive of any stance in any applied setting. The statistical principles, however, are applicable to a broad range of disciplines and readers are encouraged to follow all the worked examples with SPSS in order to absorb the basic principles.

Who shouldn't read this book?

Those already comfortable with statistics and in need of extending their knowledge to, for example, multivariate or biological statistics will not be helped by this book. Those wishing to study for an academic qualification in statistics should really be going to a text specifically targeting that qualification. And, no offence intended, but statisticians and mathematicians will probably hate this book – most squiggles are probably typographic errors.

Neither is research design a primary focus of this book. Although some references to this will be made in the first part of the book and a little more at the start of the practical sections, they are primarily there to facilitate sensible use of the tests.

It should be noted that SPSS is an expensive tool for independent researchers. If you are unable to gain access to this, you could opt to use StatsDirect, an inexpensive statistical package. To accompany this software, I have written another introductory book (Davis, 2010); it should be noted that the text and data sets are quite similar in both books.

Using the book

This is a relatively short book, and I strongly recommend that you read all of it, preferably completing the exercises as well. If this is not possible, I still strongly recommend reading the theoretical section first, before selecting a chapter and launching straight into a project. Understanding is all.

If dipping in is absolutely necessary, then at least try to read the whole chapter. Reading about multiple regression or factor analysis without a grounding in correlations and regression is unwise, to say the least.

The boxes referring to statistical theory may be skipped over by first time readers or the truly terrified, but they may in time improve your understanding of the issues.

Readers of this book who later wish to learn more about statistics, including more advanced methods, will be able to do so, confident that they have a grasp of the basic issues involved. Similarly, those who wish to use other statistical software should be able to do so after having gained useful core experience of data analysis.

It should be noted that while this book does provide some basic instruction on how to enter variables and data into SPSS, it is not devoted to SPSS in all its intricate detail. Various online tutorials and SPSS manuals (IBM, 2011) are available for this purpose.

A brief note about the author

I was never 'good at mathematics', attaining my school qualification after some retakes. Learning to use statistical tests when studying psychology as an undergraduate at the Open University, I did so by hand, spending hours working out formulae without generally seeing the point of the mathematics. As soon as I bought my first computer – a Hitachi which ran with two clunking disk drives and no hard drive – I put the formulae onto a spreadsheet and found that the real point was to know which tests to use on what data and what they were useful for, without worrying overmuch about the intermediary equations.

Working on the MSc Occupational Psychology at Birkbeck College, University of London, I deepened my knowledge of applied research and became one of those stressed people attempting to learn about factor analysis for a project at the same time as trying to master SPSS for DOS (the 'black screen' version, using typed commands). Since then, I have become involved in a wide range of research projects within diverse organisations, extending my understanding *en route*.

Acknowledgements

I would like to thank Dr George Clegg, whose experience of applied statistics has covered both academia and the defence industry. Having asked a lot of hard questions about what I intended to do, he became the first reader of the first of my books on statistical testing. He is the *eminence grise* behind the project.

Thank you also to Janine Davis and her colleagues at Bournemouth University for their assistance and cheery support.

IBM agreed to my using screenshots from SPSS. The images derive from SPSS versions 18, 19 and 20.

The responsibility for any shortcomings remains my own.

Talking point

You do not need mathematics to use statistics effectively.

Chapter 2
Descriptive statistics introduced

The focus of this book is on inferential statistics, where we make generalisations from limited amounts of data. Some knowledge of descriptive statistics is essential, however, for three reasons: it is useful in itself, it is essential preparatory work before using statistical tests, and it provides concepts underlying the use of statistical tests.

Descriptive statistics refer to both quantities and also the **shape** of the data. Before getting involved in this, we need to define the word **statistic**: as a singular noun, a statistic is a number which represents or summarises data.

The limitations of absolute data

There are times when you can just say it as it is. We have: 99 red balloons; 20,000 drug addicts; 101 Dalmatians.

Some uncontroversial statistics can also be used as figures representing groups of data. A common one is the **range**, formed from the maximum and minimum values. When given as a single statistic, this is maximum minus minimum. So if the highest value is 206 and the lowest value is 186, then the Range statistic would be 20.

Problems emerge, however, when we compare groups of data, or **data sets**. If we look at, for example, the earnings of individuals in countries of different sizes, a direct comparison may be misleading. We therefore tend to use 'averages': the description is then along the lines of the average person earning a lot in one country, and very little in another, regardless of the countries' comparative sizes.

The average

Although I am trying to avoid mathematics wherever possible, one particular statistic is a key to understanding statistics as a discipline. Relax, however: almost everyone will have heard of the concept of averages.

An average has another title, one which is longer but perhaps more meaningful: it is a measure of **central tendency**. Roughly, it defines the middle of the data being examined.

The word 'average', however, is rather a layman's term when applied to statistics. If a newspaper article claims that the average wage or salary is X pounds/dollars/roubles, what is meant? Let us look at three definitions of central tendency: the mean, the mode and the median.

The mean
The mean is an average calculated by adding together the numbers involved and then dividing the resulting number by the number of items, as in the simple example of this data set of five numbers: **2, 3, 3, 4, 8**. The sum, Σ, $= 2 + 3 + 3 + 4 + 8 = 20$. The number of items, N, $= 5$. The mean is, therefore, Σ / N: $20/5 = 4$.

The mode
The mode is the number that comes up most often. In the previous example, this would be the number 3.

The median
When the list is spread, as above, from the biggest to the smallest, then the median is the value sitting in the middle of the string of numbers. We count inwards from the string of numbers in our example, discounting first the 2 and the 8, then the outer 3 and the 4, and we are left with the number 3 in the middle as the median.

Smarter than the average bear, Boo–Boo!
To illustrate the potential use of these measures of central tendency, let us return to the newspaper article referring to 'average' pay. I don't know which statistic any given newspaper is referring to and I suspect that the reader (and possibly the writer) doesn't either. Without making a judgement, however, let us look briefly at the possibilities.

The *mean* takes the wages of all the paid workers in the city, adds them together and divides the total by the number of the workers, as if to see what one worker would have if all were equally paid. The strength of this statistic, that it takes into account the multimillionaire through to the poorest paid, can also be its weakness. Distortions created by, for example, one or two billionaires, could lead to a rather unrepresentative statistic if considered in isolation.

The *mode* may deal with this problem: most wage–earners may, for example, be administrative workers and office workers. Their wage will become the average when using the mode, but how representative is this of the earnings of the workforce in general?

The *median* may find a central value, perhaps a middle-manager's salary. This is useful, as are the other statistics, but it may not indicate the most common wage (as the mode would) nor would it take much account of the many people on poor pay and the considerable purchasing power of the very rich.

I have concentrated on the concept of central tendency (or 'average') for two reasons. The concept is very important in itself. It also demonstrates a broader truth in research, that data may be subject to different interpretations, of differing degrees of usefulness depending upon the context.

The distribution of data

Averages are just part of what is known as the distribution of data. Data can be shown in a histogram; we again use our string of numbers: 2, 3, 3, 4, 8.

Image 2.1

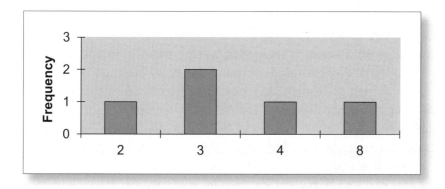

In cases where we have more data – often where the data represents a natural population, for example, automobile maximum speeds or intelligence test results – we get a distribution. One common type of distribution is the 'normal distribution', the famous bell curve (an idealised symmetrical one is shown below).

Image 2.2

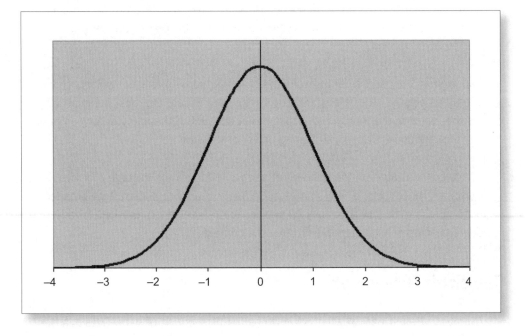

It should be noted that the curve can be sharper or more rounded, but can still retain an even distribution.

There are other types of distribution, for example, binomial, Poisson and even random, but it is the consistency or otherwise of a normal distribution which is particularly relevant when choosing between parametric and non-parametric tests, discussed in Chapter 4. Particular signs of non-normality are peaks occurring way off centre to the left or right (skew); skewed data will often be tested for significance using non-parametric tests. Another, rather unusual, occurrence is that of double peaks. Also known as bimodal distribution, the twin peaks suggest that the data contains two data samples or that there are some very interesting effects. It is suggested in the case of bimodal distribution that an examination is made of the data in question, but statistical testing of the data in its current form would not be advisable.

Regardless of whether or not the distribution is normal, various statistics are derived from the distance around the mean. Although these statistics have a considerable effect on calculations made by statistical software and are cited regularly in textbooks on statistics, we need not be overly concerned with them here. What is important is the general concept of **variance**. Variability of data around the mean – movement away from the central tendency – can be the tell-tale effect that we think we are examining or, as will be seen, it can be other factors. Although if we are examining non-normal continuous data, we may be better advised to refer to the median.

Talking point

All manner of additional statistics are churned out by statistical packages and by books on statistics. One example is kurtosis, a statistic representing the degree of flatness of the curve surrounding a distribution histogram. The author has never used this in his research and it is likely that you also never will.

Another point: there are times when descriptive statistics are all you need. Inferential statistics should only be used when there is something you want to find out (infer) from the data.

Chapter 3
Inferential statistics introduced

Inferring can mean jumping to conclusions. I hope to show that we can examine data logically and come to *reasonable* conclusions about them. In this chapter, I ask the reader to bear with me while learning some key concepts. Soon after this, we will be getting more practical.

Samples from populations

Generally, we tend to examine collections of data which are samples from a wider population. **Population** can have its usual meaning, the total number of people in a town or country, but in research terms, this often means a group of interest to us, or target group. This could be employees or students, or more narrowly, bank clerks or biology students.

As it is usually impractical to observe, question or test a whole population, for example, biology students in the whole of Canada, we usually limit ourselves to **samples** from the target population. Samples could comprise bank clerks from a selection of banks in a small town, or biology students from three colleges in different regions. Given limitations in resources, samples can be even more restricted.

Some rules of thumb have been proposed for sample size in terms of being representative of a population. One suggests that most research can be appropriately covered by sample sizes of between about 30 and 500, with 500 representing a population of millions (Roscoe, 1975). Simple, tightly controlled studies (for example, with matching pairs of participants) can have as few as 10 to 20 participants. The breaking down of samples into subsamples (for example, males/females, supervisors/workers) requires at least 30 participants per category. Multivariate techniques and also multiple regression require a sample size several times as large as the number of variables (variables are discussed in Chapter 7), preferably 10 times as many. The author would suggest that relatively small samples may be used for surveys, as long as it is recognised that there are the dangers of being rather unrepresentative and also that very real (if small) effects may be missed.

In this book, small samples of data have been chosen, with often fairly artificial characteristics, in order for the reader to enter data quickly.

Looking for an effect

If we measure an entire population, what we see is what is out there. Assuming reliable measurement, descriptive statistics would be sufficient for illustrating any perceived phenomenon. Such a phenomenon is the **effect**.

We are never sure, however, about just how representative a sample is of the population from which it is drawn. The reason for using statistical tests, at least at this introductory level, is to find out about the likely existence of an effect, or its absence, when using a sample of data. Essentially, we are interested in whether or not there are real differences between two or more sets of data or, in correlational designs, whether or not there are real relationships between them. These are effects.

Significance

For those of you who have previously been introduced to statistics and have been baffled by the 'p values' or 'null hypotheses'/'alternative hypotheses', this section is for you! *All readers should read this section carefully.*

It should be noted that I referred to *real* differences or relationships between data. With any samples, we cannot be sure about whether or not an effect is meaningful. The perceived effect could, in fact, be a chance fluctuation in the sample data or the influence of a different and perhaps unexpected effect.

The search for meaningfulness is the point of **significance testing**. Is the perceived phenomenon a fluke or not? Let us say, for example, that the same sample of people have their typing speeds measured on a Monday and on a Tuesday. We want to know if the day of the week matters – does Monday differ from Tuesday in terms of employee performance – but, we are also aware that extraneous factors (such as the journey in to work on any given day, or illness) could also affect results. The use of statistics here would be to see if there is a significant difference between the typing speeds on the two days.

Academic texts refer to the **null hypothesis**. The null hypothesis states that any perceived effect is, in fact, a matter of chance or a non-relevant factor. If, in our example, any differences in performance are likely to be down to a cold or a traffic jam, then *the null hypothesis is accepted*. In everyday terms, the result is *not significant*.

If, however, the effect is clear-cut – regardless of a few people having a bad day, there is a clear difference between the performances on Monday and on Tuesday – then, academically speaking, *the null hypothesis is rejected*, or *the alternative hypothesis* (the alternative to chance fluctuation) *is accepted*. In everyday terms, the result is *significant*.

I have mentioned these definitions of hypotheses as you will encounter them in text books, academic reporting and, sometimes, in statistical software results. When reporting in applied research, however, and for your own sanity, the fluke/chance/interfering factors/null result can be referred to as *not significant*. The 'real' effect can be referred to as a *significant* effect or result.

But why have I discussed these issues in what appears to be the wrong order, starting with the non-significant (null hypothesis) result and only then the sought-after significant result? Essentially, tests of significance are concerned with the likelihood of an effect being the result of extraneous factors. These calculations of variance about the mean, like the computers running them, do not share your enthusiasm for that significant effect; they are seeking out the *probability of a chance result*.

There is a lot of theory about probability, starting from simple branching – heads and tails – through to mind-exploding calculations. All that you need to consider here is the question, 'is the effect significant or a matter of irrelevant fluctuation?'

Which takes us to the *p* value. The **p value** of a test is the measure of significance. It tells us the *likelihood of a result being insignificant!*

The percentage of the *p* value is the calculated chance of your test result being a fluke. Let us say, for example, that the precise *p* value is .03 This means that there is a three in a hundred chance that the result has emerged from irrelevant fluctuations. It therefore seems rather likely that your result is significant.

Try not to get carried away, however, by starting to talk about 97% success rates or anything like that. Stick to the .03 What it really means is that, according to the statistical calculations, if you tried the test on a hundred samples, then there is a 3% chance that the data could yield a fluke result. Yes, it looks good, but your result could still be that three-in-a-hundred irrelevance.

A corollary of this is that if you used 100 samples, there is a likelihood that you could end up with three misleading results. There is a practical side to this: if you run a series of tests, 'dredging', a temptation when dealing with a complicated data set, the chance of some of them being fluke results increases considerably. (A false positive like this is what is known as a Type 1 error. A Type 2 error, by the way, is a false negative, where you miss what is in fact a significant finding.)

This is why replication of results is often recommended in academic journals and – if the result is at all important to your organisation – it may well be sensible in practice. (The issue of 'reliability' will be raised occasionally in this book, but the reader may profit from in-depth discussions of this issue in books devoted to research in general; or for a quick and free read, try Roberts et al, 2006.)

A high *p* value, for example, .337 is highly suggestive of a fluke. The highest number *p* value is 1. A value of .333 informs us that there is a one in three chance of your results being due to a random or irrelevant fluctuation. Although you could replicate this, it does not seem worth it. But what level of significance is worth considering?

Frequently we do not refer to a precise *p* value. Computers often and researchers much more regularly, refer to the *p* value in more general terms: *p* is smaller than something. This is sometimes called the **critical value**. Commonly quoted critical values are $p < 0.05$, $p < 0.01$ and $p < 0.001$ respectively. The chances of a fluke result are calculated as being less than five in a hundred (5%), less than one in a hundred and less than one in a thousand. The critical values $p < .02$ and $p < .005$ are not unheard of. All refer to the likelihood of any variance being a matter of chance or unexpected factors.

Although it is quite common to merely 'read off' the p values or critical values from the computerised results, some would argue that the researcher should decide upon an acceptable level of significance *before* using the statistical tests. The point is that there should be an acceptable level of risk (or academic rigour). While $p < .05$ may be acceptable to a psychologist using a sample of twenty students, where it may be difficult to find a significant result and where the experiment can be replicated easily next year, a business may, in some cases, want the chance of an error to be less than $p < .01$. An aircraft manufacturer, however, may want $p < .0001$, with replications. In any case, a well-aired controversy is whether or not the researcher should decide on what is acceptable *after* looking at the results.

Statistical theory – the horror, the horror!

p values and critical values

p value – this is a precise number relating to a test result's significance, such as .03

critical value – this is how the p value compares to a level of significance, for example, $p < .05$

I have suggested in this book that deciding on the required significance level, the critical value method, is good practice. It sets the results of the test in the context of the type of research being undertaken.

An opposing view does exist. The p value allows people to draw their own conclusions. If, for example, .03 is the p value emerging from the statistical test, you may choose to read it as significant at $p < .05$, while another reader of the report who believes .01 to be more suitable is free to consider the result as non-significant. If you merely report the result as significant to your preferred critical value, for example, $p < .05$, without offering the p value, the other reader would be unable to do this.

However, the downside of using the p value method is losing the rigour of having set a preferred critical value. Or at least, the reader would not know if you had or not.

If you wish to stay on the good side of the holders of both of these opinions, then the answer is to cite both the critical value that you set (for example, $p < .01$) and also the p value itself. For example, '$p = .03$; not significant at $p < .01$'

A final point when deciding upon which level of significance is acceptable is the question of **one-tailed** and **two-tailed** hypotheses. A one-tailed hypothesis means that you know from the start, because of the nature of the exercise, in which direction the effect is going. A two-tailed hypothesis means that you can not be sure in which direction a significant result would run. (These terms relate to variance from the mean to only one end of the distribution versus possible variance to both sides.) For example, if you are already sure that the typing speeds are worse on Mondays than on Tuesdays and have good reasons for this being the case (and the test confirms this), if the statistical test indicated that $p < .01$, you could accept that there is less than a 1% chance of a fluke result. If, however, you have not been committed to which day is likely to result in faster typing, a chance result is twice as likely (there is variance to either side of the mean). So, in the interests of rigour, you double the critical value, accepting a more modest $p < .02$ two-tailed. (In academic reporting, you would refer to the result being significant at $p < .01$ one-tailed or significant at $p < .02$ two-tailed. In non-academic reports, you would just quote the level of significance as being smaller than .01 or .02.)

Effect size

So the concept of significance is about the likelihood of an effect's existence. Effect size, however, is about how far the effect accounts for the variance, the swing away from the mean. It is possible to have results of quite high significance but relatively low effect size. In such cases, the effect only contributes very little to the variance. Perhaps other effects have been missed, or perhaps there is experimental 'noise', random factors introduced into the environment. In practical terms, this may mean that, while we can be fairly sure of an effect's existence, it may be of little practical relevance.

In your encounters with SPSS, you will meet various statistics which represent effect size, including r2 and partial eta squared. Sometimes, you will come across effect sizes which account for a large proportion of the effect.

Let us say, for example, that we are examining the relationship between two sets of data. The correlation coefficient, r, is .639 which we square to find the effect size r^2 (.639 * .639). The effect size is .408, almost 41% of the variance. Any more than 10% of the variance is considered to be a large effect size.

At other times, however, results will be significant but with a negligible effect size. In order to report on the relative size, whether or not the effect can be called large, small or middling in size, some value judgements should be made relating to the context of the observations. Looking at the findings of previous similar research is particularly recommended. However, if in doubt, rules of thumb are provided in various sections of the book.

Talking point

If you already have the data for a whole population, you don't need to infer: a population is already representative of itself. You may, however, use inferential tests to compare (or contrast) one part of the population with another. They may differ in more ways than just the measure in which you are interested, so the test can allow for fluctuations.

Chapter 4
On the nature of numbers

An important concern in quantitative research is that of the 'criterion problem'. The criterion is the subject of measurement. If the criterion, that which is being measured, is irrelevant or inappropriate for the test being used, then no estimations of significance can be considered valid. We have built on a house of cards. Although the accuracy of measurement is more a matter of research design and is, therefore, not our primary concern in this book, the issue of data being appropriate for running particular tests must be discussed.

Different tests carry different assumptions about the data they analyse. Such assumptions become particularly important when deciding whether or not to use parametric tests (to be discussed shortly) and in considering the quantification of qualitative statistics (yes!) in Chapter 8.

The nature of numbers is fundamental to using statistical tests. Running tests with inappropriate data can lead to a mass of apparently significant (or insignificant) results which are, in fact, meaningless. This sort of error is easily made and computer software packages in many cases will not be any more aware of the problem than you are. This is, of course, a good reason for examining data before testing, including using descriptive charts. You must ensure that the data you input is appropriate. In most cases this includes using the same type of numbers in all data sets used.

One way of conceptualising the different types of data used is to consider its texture. Is it finely chopped or coarse? Here, I want to look at three types of measurement data: continuous, ordinal and categorical.

At the fine end we have **continuous** data (referred to as **Scale** by SPSS). This exists as a run of information which has 'natural' proportions. Distances, seconds and uninterrupted lists of financial value (where they are not banded) are of this kind. In some research reports you may see this subdivided into ratio data and interval data. Ratio data runs from zero (for example, 0, 1 dollar, 2 dollars, 3 dollars...), while interval data can start above zero (as in typing speeds per minute: 30 wpm, 31 wpm, 32 wpm, 33 wpm and so on). In terms of statistical calculations in this book, there is no difference between ratio and interval types of continuous data. Continuous data is usually the grist for parametric tests.

At times, you may be unsure as to whether or not you are dealing with truly continuous data. Ask yourself if doubling (or halving) a given amount will give a meaningful result. If it does, it is truly continuous.

IQ results appear to be continuous data, but are you sure that somebody with an IQ of 140 has exactly twice the measured intelligence of somebody tested as having an IQ of 70? Similarly, the idea of doubling or halving a Likert scale rating from a questionnaire (see below) is a dubious one:

Table 4.1

1	2	3	4	5	6
Very unsatisfied	Unsatisfied	Indifferent	Satisfied	Very satisfied	Ecstatic

More coarsely grained numbers, measurably of a different size from each other but not truly continuous, are usually subsumed within **ordinal** numbers. IQ and most Likert scales truly belong here (unless the latter are very well calibrated, but Item Response Theory is well outside the remit of this book – see, for example, Embretson and Reise, 2000). The same would be true of an arbitrary set of prices ($1.40, $2.99), pay bandings ($20,000–$30,000, $31,000–$40,000) and various other measures which are not strictly continuous.

Ordinal data is so-called because it can be ordered, or ranked. There is a quantitative difference between numbers – one is bigger than another – even if they are not 'smooth' and cannot be arithmetically manipulated like continuous numbers. Such 'lumpy data' – for example 3, 13, 23, 25, 60, 80 – are generally examined by non-parametric tests (see below), which puts them into a rank order of magnitude.

At the far end of our data continuum is **categorical** data, otherwise known as **nominal** (in SPSS Variable View) or **qualitative** data. My old physics teacher referred to the concept as 'elephants and telegraph poles' when referring to entities which do not mix. I can't remember the precise context, or almost anything else I was taught in physics, but this concept of exclusive differentiation stuck. *Each category must be exclusive: each observation is counted up to make the* **frequency** *within one category.*

Categorical data can be **dichotomous** (male/female, yes/no and so on). It can also include classifications arbitrarily decided by the researcher; examples could include types of employee (manual, clerical, managerial), people holding specific viewpoints (hostile to a concept, approving, indifferent) or even agglomerations of ranges of numbers (well-paid, comfortable, in dire straits).

This qualitative choice raises an issue which should be considered throughout your data analysis or research. There needs to be a theory behind your decision making. I do not mean academic theories (although these may be considered in order to make sense of what you are doing), but some form of rationale. Without this you may, in effect, be doing something similar to just putting data into the computer and hoping that what emerges is meaningful – which it usually isn't.

(Mixed data, including dichotomous, or binary data, can be subjected to logistic regression, but that takes us outside this introductory volume – see, for example, Hosmer and Lemeshow, 2000.)

Parametric versus non-parametric data

In both tests of differences between data sets and also tests involving correlations (relationships between data), the test user will sometimes discover a choice between using parametric and non-parametric tests.

Parametric tests are used when certain **assumptions** are made about the parameters (the limits and nature) of the data. These tests should only be used if the assumptions are met. Data should be *continuous*, as in being naturally proportioned, should form a *normal distribution* and, if the samples are of unequal size, should contain *homogeneity of variance*. Essentially, homogeneity of variance means that numbers in the data sets should be of the same proportion (*not*, for example, 2, 3, 4, 5, 3 tested against 23, 28, 33, 46, 30, 43).

As a rule of thumb, experimental and quasi-experimental data (see the analysis of differences chapter), when continuous, may be suitable candidates for parametric tests. A strict test of data suitability, looking for normal distribution, is provided by the Shapiro–Wilk test for sample sizes of less than 50 and Kolmogorov–Smirnov for larger samples.

If the assumptions are not met but you are still using measurable data, then you should use **non-parametric tests**. Non-parametric tests are designed to ignore the lop-sidedness of data. If, for example, we had the numbers 16, 15, 13, 32, 4, 4, 3, a parametric test would certainly be much affected by the far-flung number (assuming that 32 is an outlier rather than an error). A non-parametric test would rank the data:

32 (1st), 16 (2nd), 15 (3rd), 13 (4th), 4 (5th equal), 4 (5th equal), 3 (7th), which would mean that the abnormally large number would not exercise undue influence.

As would be usual when using statistical tests, you would check your descriptive statistics first. Is the outlier (32, in this case) a legitimate part of your data set? If it is a matter of poor data entry, it is appropriate to alter this. If you decide that this was an uncharacteristic performance (maybe the respondent had an unfair advantage), you may consider deleting that record (although such a decision should be carefully considered and recorded). If the outlier is legitimate, a non-parametric test can use the data without being unduly influenced by its extreme nature.

Statistical theory – put your fingers in your ears and sing

Parametric tests and non-parametric tests
Parametric tests – these focus on variability around the mean. They also take into account 'error', which can mean both the effects of variables that you are not testing (for example, individual differences between cases) and also unknown variability. The predicted variability is divided by the error to give a ratio. This gives the test statistic, *t* as in the T tests and the *F* ratio as in analysis of variance (ANOVA). A large ratio, predicted variability being much greater than error, means that a result is less likely to be a result of chance or alternative variables and more likely to be considered significant (that is, rejecting the null hypothesis).

The mean is the important average here and should be part of your reporting.

Non-parametric tests – these do not examine the raw data, but rank the data according to the scores' relative sizes. They are insensitive to big differences between scores and non-normality.

The median is the most relevant average when non-parametric data is either continuous or ordinal.

Talking point

Many books recommend the use of parametric tests wherever possible. They are considered to be 'more powerful' than their non-parametric alternatives and should, therefore, be able to detect significant results which may otherwise be missed. The choice, however, is highly dependent upon conditions. As most data analysis conditions in everyday research are not textbook examples, non-parametric tests are more likely to be used. In any case, when confronted with data suitable for parametric tests, non-parametric tests generally produce very similar results.

Chapter 5
Data entry in SPSS

Data entry with Excel and other spreadsheet formats (for example StatsDirect)

For the sake of simplicity, let us say that you have two small sets of numbers you wish to analyze: 40, 30, 45, 60, 45 and 50, 40, 45, 50, 43. In Excel, you just type them in two adjacent columns, preferably with a descriptive header in the cells above them. This would happen regardless of whether or not the participants were the same in both conditions. You will notice shortly that, when the participants in each data set are different from each other, SPSS is structured very differently.

Entering scores with SPSS

In practice using SPSS, you should name your variables first. For learning purposes, however, we start here with how the scores are entered.

Using SPSS, it really matters if your data represents a within-subjects or between-subjects design (see the analysis of differences chapter for more on research design). If the participants are the same (within-subjects), multiple score columns are needed:

Table 5.1

1	40	50
2	30	40
3	45	45
3	60	50
5	45	43

Essentially, this data represents five people, each with two sets of scores. However, where the participants are different on all occasions (between-subjects), then all of the scores are in the same column. **The basic rule for SPSS is that each row must represent just one case (or person).**

Table 5.2

1	40	1
2	30	1
3	45	1
4	60	1
5	45	1
6	50	2
7	40	2
8	45	2
9	50	2
10	43	2

Here, we have ten different people. They are in two separate categories, however, and the right-hand column represents a **grouping variable**, for example, Experimental Group = 1, Control Group = 2.

You will also note in both cases a running total on the left. This is in order to keep track of what you are doing when manipulating larger data sets.

Variable View

In practice, using the SPSS **Data Editor**, you generally start by creating the variables. This reduces the risk of putting data in the wrong columns. Variables are created in **Variable View** (accessible via a tab at the bottom of the program).

In Variable View, the variables' attributes are shown in columns starting with the working name (corresponding to the column heading **Name**) on the left.

Image 5.1

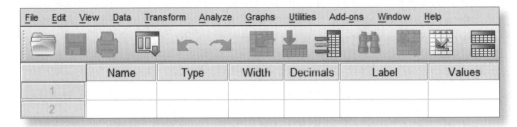

With both of the above sets of numbers, you would first enter under Name something like 'Case', which is an abbreviation, without gaps between words, which would then appear at the head of your data column in Data View but will not appear in the program's output. (Its full name, under Label, will be something like 'Case number'.)

In the within-subjects example, the name on the next row down would be something like Experiment, and the next row down would be named Control; the same people having been participants under two conditions. So the format in Variable View would look as follows (the other column settings are defaults):

Image 5.2

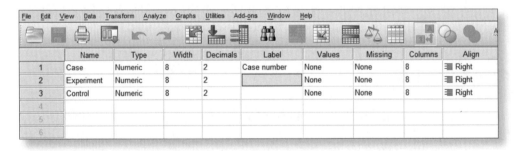

It is suggested that you save this file with a name such as 'Same'. We will enter the data shortly.

In the between-subjects example, the next row would be called Score or Result, with the following row, the grouping variable, being called something like

Condition. The changes to the Decimals, Label and Values columns will become clearer shortly. It is suggested that you save this file with a name such as 'Different'.

Image 5.3

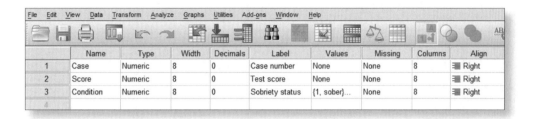

	Name	Type	Width	Decimals	Label	Values	Missing	Columns	Align
1	Case	Numeric	8	0	Case number	None	None	8	Right
2	Score	Numeric	8	0	Test score	None	None	8	Right
3	Condition	Numeric	8	0	Sobriety status	{1, sober}...	None	8	Right
4									

The next column is **Type**, which is preset to numeric values but can be set to string (for names) or other settings, including date and currency. The numeric values are pre-set at 2 decimal places. As this becomes irritating when dealing with integers, you may want to set this to 0 in some cases; click on the dots to the right of the relevant cell. If your output is going to use currency, other than dollars, you need to go to the menu at the top of the Data Editor to find Edit/Options/Currency. Here you can define a prefix or suffix (for example GBP) which can then be used by clicking on the cell dots as before.

Width refers to the width of the columns in Data View; the default being 8. As with the next column, this can be set in the *Type* column.

Decimals may often be set to zero, as integers become an unsightly nuisance when forever trailing places (1.00, 2.00, 3.00...).

Label is the full name of the data, which will appear in your output. This can contain gaps and for better comprehensibility should read like Case number, Experimental condition, Control condition and so on.

Values are used with *grouping variables*. Words are given to the code numbers. If you click the dots to the right of the cell, you reach a dialog box. Let us say that your condition was 'sobriety status', you could insert 1 in the *value* field in the dialog box and 'sober' in the *label* field,

Image 5.4

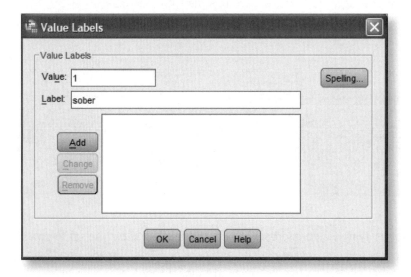

then press 'Add'.

Do the same with 2 and the word 'drinking', which should give you this:

Image 5.5

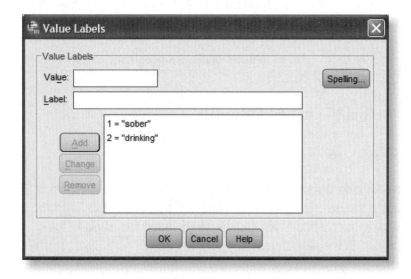

When you are finished, press 'OK'.

This means that the output from any analysis will provide the names of the grouping variables instead of the original numbers given.

Missing – While SPSS allows for missing values in its calculations ('system-missing values'), you may wish to have certain values ignored ('user-missing values'). You specify which values you want as missing and allocate a number such as –9.

Columns – the width of columns you can *see* in Data View.

Align – Cells can be aligned *Left, Right* and *Center*. The default settings are right for numbers and left for strings of letters.

Measure – 'scale' is the default for numbers, although 'ordinal' is available, as is 'nominal', which would be used in the case of strings (words). This is necessary when using SPSS charts.

Role – this appears in more recent editions of SPSS and relates to the automation of tasks in some procedures. 'Input' classifies the variable as an independent variable or predictor (the distinction between these two terms is discussed in the chapter on the analysis of differences). 'Output' is for a dependent variable or criterion. A 'Both' option is also available. This only sets defaults on some dialog boxes and is not essential.

Data View

Again, this is accessible via a tab at the bottom of the program.

If you have already created variables in Variable View, then these variables should appear at the top of the columns when you move to Data View.

Looking at the 'Same' file, enter the data from the first data set.

Image 5.6

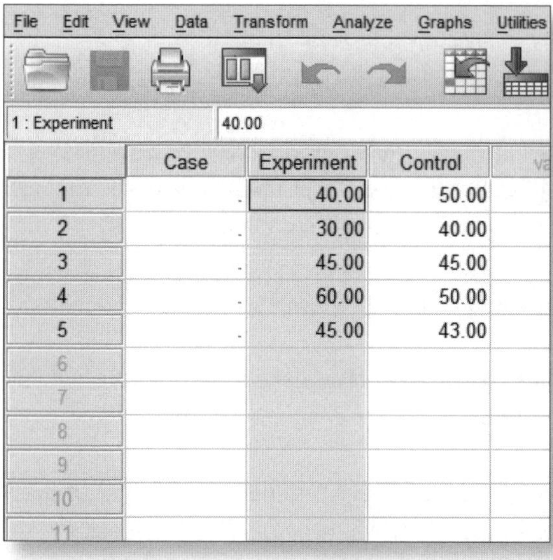

	Case	Experiment	Control	va
1	.	40.00	50.00	
2	.	30.00	40.00	
3	.	45.00	45.00	
4	.	60.00	50.00	
5	.	45.00	43.00	
6				
7				
8				
9				
10				
11				

File Edit View Data Transform Analyze Graphs Utilities

1 : Experiment   40.00

To get rid of those pesky zeroes, you can go back to Variable View and adjust the decimals for Experiment and Control to zero. Remember to save the 'Same' file.

Now, on the 'Different' file, enter the scores and the grouping variables. And save.

Image 5.7

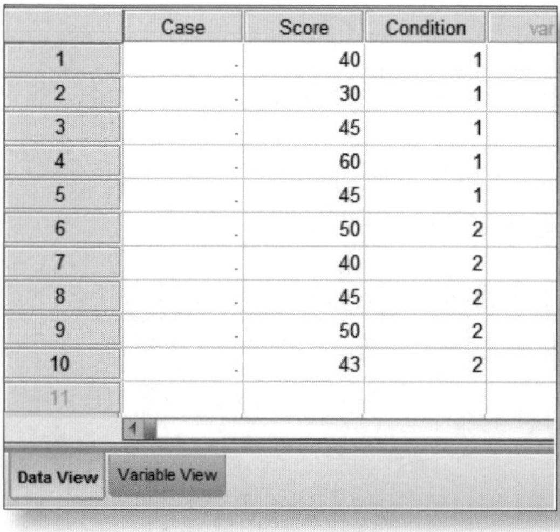

	Case	Score	Condition	var
1	.	40	1	
2	.	30	1	
3	.	45	1	
4	.	60	1	
5	.	45	1	
6	.	50	2	
7	.	40	2	
8	.	45	2	
9	.	50	2	
10	.	43	2	
11				

Data View   Variable View

Note that I have not suggested typing in the case numbers (1, 2, 3 ...). This is because with large data sets you may want to automate this (type 3,000, 3,001, 3,002 – no, I don't think so).

To automate case numbers, ensure that the scores already exist in Data View and then highlight the empty 'Case' column, as in the image above. Then go to Variable View to adjust the variable Case to Decimals = 0 and ensure that 'Case number' is entered under the Label column. Then use *Transform/Compute Variable*, typing the word Case into the top left box of the Compute Variable dialog ('Target Variable'). A Type and Label icon will appear underneath; select this and type 'Case number' and press 'Continue'. Then in the main Compute Variable dialog box, type $CASENUM into the Numeric Expression field and then press 'OK'.

Image 5.8

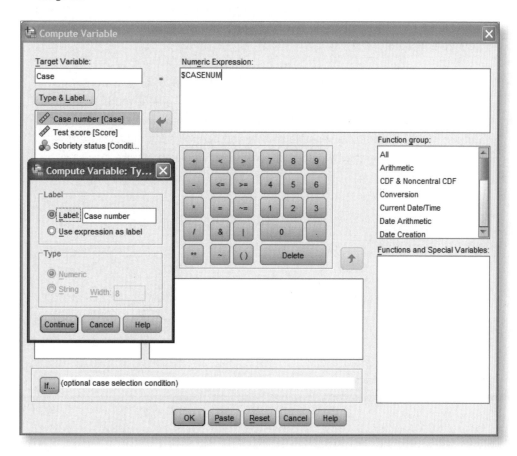

At the moment, Sobriety status has a scale symbol attached to it. This should be changed, adjusting the 'Measure' variable to Nominal. If there were a range of rankable values – for example, very fast, fast, medium and so on – then this would be Ordinal.

When you return to *Data* View you should see the running total in place.

Do note the status bar at the bottom of the program. It may say that the processor is ready or, when performing a calculation, it may monitor progress.

Talking point

Try to get into the habit of creating variables first in Variable View before going to Data View to enter your data. Create meaningful variable names. The clearer your notions are of the variables you are examining, the easier your analysis when life gets complicated!

Also, remember to save regularly, as a freeze can lose a lot of your work. And use clear file names, including new files using 'save as' where you have created subsets of data. When updating data sets, the use of file names with dates or edition numbers would be sensible so that you can roll back in case of errors. Mistakes happen in lengthy pieces of work; a well-stocked archive may save a lot of time later....

Chapter 6
Data analysis in practice

Data analysis within the research process

Before continuing further into the details of conducting data analysis, it is advisable to take a step back and look at why we conduct statistical tests. Although this book is primarily devoted to choosing, using and interpreting statistical tests, data analysis should be seen within the context of research – for very practical reasons.

We should be clear about what is to be researched. If this is not the case, then interpretations may be marred by reliance on automated answers and a desire to 'press the button' to see what happens. Intelligent data analysis should bear in mind the nature of what is being investigated, as will become particularly clear when we discuss factor analysis in Chapter 9.

Similarly, research design should be clear from the outset. One reason is obvious: it is important to measure the thing that you are interested in measuring. Another reason tends to emerge only later, as researchers come to grips with the collection of data and its analysis.

The acceptability of research methods is frequently cited as a problem in both academic and applied research. As well as the more widely publicised ethical issues, you need to consider how effective your data collection methods are. I have lost count of the times I have seen researchers having to alter their projects, apparently surprised to find that busy professionals (and most other people) do not want to fill in their 60-question surveys! Similarly, I never fail to find useful ideas coming out of trial runs ('pilots'). Do them.

Design problems have a knock-on effect on data analysis. Radical alterations of surveys, for example, mean that different data sets have to be made compatible with each other, often needing data transformation. Other problems can include having too much data: who will examine this and how much time will be available?

If researchers collate information from interviews for qualitative analysis, they need to agree on what can reasonably be subsumed into categories, both on theoretical grounds and for the purposes of analysis. ('30 people said they hated X, 26 people were indifferent to X and 1 said it was beneath his contempt.' '40 used foul language, although 7 of them seemed to use the words as technical descriptions.')

Clearly, some consideration of data analysis requirements should be made in advance.

However, the purpose of conducting research should be the driving force,

Research design

This book is primarily about statistical testing, with particular emphasis on using SPSS. It would be impracticable to refer to research design in great detail here, as each research field is rather different in its focus and there are usually plenty of books which cover research design for particular disciplines. For example, a book on business statistics (certainly marketing) should spend a considerable amount of time looking at survey design, calibration, internal reliability and so on (see Sekaran and Bougie, 2009). It would do no harm, however, to outline core research design issues, with some comments upon their effects on data analysis.

One thing to consider is whether or not a design is experimental. Before non-scientists rush off to the next paragraph, it is worth noting that people conduct experiments in everyday settings. A manager, for example, can randomly allocate some workers to a training course and can compare their performance with another group, the control group, who are not given training. The type of training is a **variable** (also known in SPSS as a factor). The manager has manipulated this variable and, by examining its effect on something measurable, the manager has performed an experiment.

Random allocation of the subjects (in the case of humans in particular, these are also called participants), is generally a sign of a true experiment. You will find from reading more about research design (for example, Davies, 2007; Creswell, 2008), that experiments can be made more rigorous. Drugs are often tested, for example, using a double-blind procedure (neither the patient nor the administrator knows which drug is being administered). Experimental subjects are often chosen according to whether or not they have prior experience of a particular experience.

In many cases, however, time and resources mean that we are less rigorous rather than more so. We can still conduct **quasi-experiments**. One example is the choice of fixed groups, for example, looking at the differences between men and women on a particular measure – the variable apparently being manipulated is gender – or in our manager's case, different types of worker being allocated to different courses. Each course, or no course at all, is a **condition**; this is also referred to in SPSS as a **level**, as it is a level of the variable/factor.

You will also come across cases where no positive action has occurred at all, but data is looked at retrospectively. Perhaps the training courses took place last year and you decide to examine the available performance data. It is still possible to identify one or more 'experimental' groups and a 'control' group. You will be examining historical data as if an experiment has taken place.

The good news from a data analysis perspective is that experiments and quasi-experiments can be analysed similarly. Usually, we will want to see the effect of our variable in different conditions; the chapter on the analysis of differences is probably your first port of call.

Within experiments and quasi-experiments, however, a major design issue is that of **between-subjects design** versus **within-subjects design** (within subjects is referred to in SPSS as 'repeated measures').

On the whole, within-subjects designs are superior: apart from being more efficient by using less people, they iron out individual differences. The effect of differences between people can confound the effect that you wish to examine.

However, within-subjects designs do suffer from **order effects**. We can return to the training example to illustrate one type of order effect: we can not be sure if the effects of training are not confounded with individual or organisational maturation. So we may wish to examine the effects of people doing no training for a while and then doing the training later. Maybe we will be lucky and find cases of some training courses which took place later on in the careers of comparable people. So we have A followed by B (the same people in training and in a post-training phase) and also B followed by A (no training, followed by training – presumably we would get our performance data later on).

Even where order effects do not make things impossible, you would still want to minimise them where possible by careful allocation of subjects to different combinations of conditions such as A followed by B and B followed by A. You may want to look up research designs such as completely randomised design, randomised block design, Latin square design and factorial design (see Sekaran and Bougie, 2009).

As within-subjects is a generally worthwhile design to choose where possible, this comes before between-subjects in the presentation of tests in this book.

However, if in our training example we are unable to find people who trained later, we are unable to continue with our design. We can not reasonably 'untrain' our individuals, so we are unable to compare the same people under different conditions in both directions. Similar problems relate to exposure to experimental materials which again could contaminate results (those interested in educational tests, for example, could consider parallel tests – see, for example, Maughan et al, 2009).

The main advantage of between-subjects design is, of course, freedom from order effects, although we are still not free from contamination effects such as different times of day, organisational and maturational factors. The main disadvantage is, of course, individual differences. Although statistical procedures try to allow for these, the researcher should try to minimise their effects wherever possible, as the statistical tests can only do so much. Consider large samples to even out differences. Again, look at randomisation techniques.

Another possibility is the **matched/paired design**. Instead of the same person under different conditions, different people would be chosen as being similar in the most relevant attribute(s). In our training example the manager could find people with very similar backgrounds in another branch of the same organisation where the same courses were conducted but at a somewhat different time. We could then have A followed by B in one branch and B followed by A in another branch. If the participants and organisational conditions are similar in appropriate ways, you can adopt a matched/paired design and can test as if in a same-subjects experiment.

Correlational design is also frequently used. Here we are interested in the *relationships* between phenomena rather than the differences between them. This can be applied to two or more variables. Please note that, by itself, correlational design does not indicate cause and effect. If we have, for example, a clear relationship between the effects of a training course and motivation, it may be tempting to claim that the course increased motivation. But the converse is also possible: the more motivated trainees may have been more inclined to use their training effectively than their colleagues. As well as direct problems in interpretation there are also what are known as mediating variables: some variables are related to the ones you are interested in and are sometimes called confounding variables. However, by the time you have considered correlations (Chapter 9) and factorial analysis of variance (Chapter 10), these will not worry you (well all right, they will worry you less).

The desire to look at correlations can arise from a range of situations. It may arise from observations: something may look similar to something else and you may wish to see if the relationship is a significant one. Straightforward correlations may be most appropriate. You may wonder to what extent different factors affect an outcome; here, you would probably use multiple regression. Within an experimental situation, you may wonder if one effect interacts with another; this is where a factorial ANOVA comes into its own, with a choice between within-subjects, between-subjects and mixed designs.

Comparative design is a peculiar beast. This looks at naturally occurring groups. Instead of allocating persons or things to groups, we see how many cases fall within each of two or more categories and test to see if the differences in frequencies are meaningfully different from chance.

This design clearly has no relationship with experiments, in that we do not use measured data and we do not allocate persons or things to groups. We just look at the frequency of categorical data.

As with correlations, naturalistic observations may lead to this form of analysis. The different reactions to a survey, preferred habitats or leisure activities, can all be counted and placed in categories.

Also, as with correlations, relationships between variables can be examined, but here in the shape of the Chi Square test of association where variables are examined in a grid format. Two variables are juxtaposed against two or more variables in a set of frequency boxes. The test examines the interrelationship between the two variables.

You will often be able to use qualitative analysis for a variety of more general research purposes. I used to gather comments from the end of otherwise structured surveys, or from interviews, and collated those comments which were similar into categories. Again, I could look at relationships between categories, for example by sub-dividing the attitudinal reactions according to gender.

Generally speaking, the relevant tests are those in the chapter on qualitative analysis. However, qualitative differences may also be studied over time. Although **longitudinal design** effects can be measured indirectly using other methods (for example, 'before and after' studies of measurable data), one highly useful set of techniques comes under the general heading of **'time until events'**, also known as **survival analysis**. Like most observational studies this also works by keeping a frequency count, but this time of the occurrence of events over time. As will be shown (Chapter 11) this has a bearing on a wide range of problems: from the commonly known analysis of medical effectiveness to the effects of training, patterns of reoffending and any other countable events that can be tracked over time.

One way of structuring data analysis

Assuming that research design has been considered, we now turn to conducting data analysis. In practice, people find different ways of approaching problems. What is suggested below is just one way of structuring your work.

Decide what it is you want to measure first – have a rationale

Ideally, you will have designed the data collation yourself, thus meeting your knowledge needs and making it easy to analyse. Often, however, you are given the data and it is left to you to analyse it. In either case, you need to decide what you want to discriminate between, categorise or compare. As I hope will be quite clear, just inputting data and hoping the 'results' are significant is likely to mislead you and everybody else.

Look at the descriptive statistics

There are two main ways of looking at data, numerical and graphical. For the moment, let us see how SPSS allows you to examine the numbers.

Comparing continuous data – within-subjects

Do note that, just as in data entry, SPSS views same-subject and between-subject data differently.

First, open the 'Same' file. From the menu at the top, use *Analyze/Descriptive Statistics/Descriptives*. This provides a basic comparison between the two conditions for the same set of people. (Notice the symbols by the variables; the rule denotes that the measure chosen in Variable View is 'Scale'.) Transfer the two conditions, Experiment and Control, to the 'Variable(s)' box and then press 'OK'.

Image 6.1

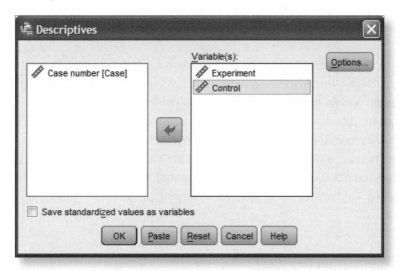

Image 6.2

Descriptive Statistics

	N	Minimum	Maximum	Mean	Std. Deviation
Experiment	5	30	60	44.00	10.840
Control	5	40	50	45.60	4.393
Valid N (listwise)	5				

The SPSS Viewer makes its first appearance and we see the above data, including a difference in the mean averages of the data for the two conditions. If we had

Part One

used 'options' we could have added additional statistics, such as the variance and the sums of the two different sets of scores.

Do note, however, that if dealing with non-parametric data, the median is preferred. For this purpose, use *Analyze/Descriptive Statistics/Frequencies*. In the Frequencies dialog box, transfer the 'Experiment' and 'Control' variables to the box on the right just as you did with Descriptives. Then press the 'Statistics' button on the right, to select 'Median'. The output should tell you the number of cases in each condition and the medians for each (here, 45 in both cases).

Comparing continuous data – between-subjects

Just as SPSS requires different input of data for between-subjects design, so the analysis of data is rather different, using category or 'grouping variables'.

Go to the 'Different' file. From the menu at the top, use *Analyze/Compare Means/ Means*. Highlight 'Score' (or 'Results' and so on) and put it in the 'Dependent List' by pressing the appropriate arrow button (the results are the 'dependent variable', or target or criterion, that which is being measured as the outcome of the study). Then highlight Condition, Sobriety status or whatever is the relevant categorical variable in order to put it in the 'Independent List' (the 'independent variable' or predictor, the variable manipulated to achieve the results). We may also look at the medians by clicking 'Options' on the dialog box; following on with 'Continue'.

Image 6.3

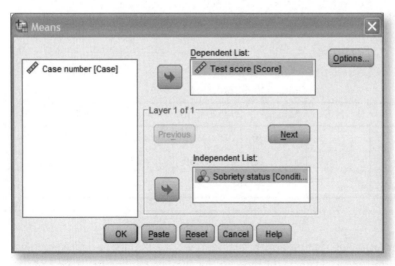

(The symbol beside the sobriety variable is for the 'Nominal' measure.) Do note the 'Next' button. This allows 'layering', the introduction of another variable with which to break up the data (gender is a typical variable for layering).

Then press 'OK'.

After a summary of the overall data, you will see the two categories and also the combined sample, with read-outs for the mean, the number of cases, the Standard Deviation (*SD*) and the median.

More extensive information is provided by *Analyze/Descriptive Statistics/Explore*

You will generally want to report at least the means for your data sets. Large differences between the means often indicate significant differences between data sets.

Comparing ordinal and nominal data

Here we consider ordinal data with relatively few categories (for example, very fast, fast, medium, slow, very slow). Ordinal data with many categories could be treated as continuous data (and should later be tested for significance using non-parametric tests) or can be recoded into more restricted categories.

Recoding

Let us recode our current measurement data. We could use *Transform/Recode into Different Variables* (safer than overlaying your original data) or *Transform/Visual Binning*. The Visual Binner, known in some editions of SPSS as the Visual Bander, is available in both the full and student versions of SPSS and we show a brief example of its use here.

Please open the 'Different' file. Select *Transform/Visual Binning*. Put Test score (Score) into 'Variables to Bin', then 'Continue'.

Image 6.4

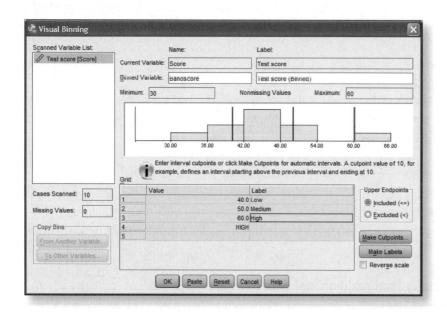

All that we have done here is to write a new variable name, Bandscore, next to 'Binned Variable' with a new label, Banded Test Score. In the grid, we have selected a score of 40 as the highest point for the band we have called 'Low', 50 for 'Medium' and 60 for 'High'. (Ignore the 'HIGH' value; it is a default.) Then 'OK'.

Image 6.5

	Case	Score	Condition	Bandscore	Gender	var
1	1	40	1	1	1	
2	2	30	1	1	1	
3	3	45	1	2	2	
4	4	60	1	3	2	
5	5	45	1	2	2	
6	6	50	2	2	2	
7	7	40	2	1	1	
8	8	45	2	2	2	
9	9	50	2	2	1	
10	10	43	2	2	1	
11						

Data View | Variable View

As you can see from Data View a new variable has been created, Bandscore. This variable has the number 1 for the lowest score, 2 for the medium score and 3 for the highest, but banding names that were chosen (in this case, Low, Medium and High) will appear in any analytical output. Also, we have added a new variable, Gender; in Data View, create 'Gender' as the name and label, with Values of 1 for Female and 2 for Male. Enter the numbers, as above, in Data View.

Now that we have recoded, we can examine the data using *Analyze/Descriptive Statistics/Crosstabs* (cross-tabulation).

Image 6.6

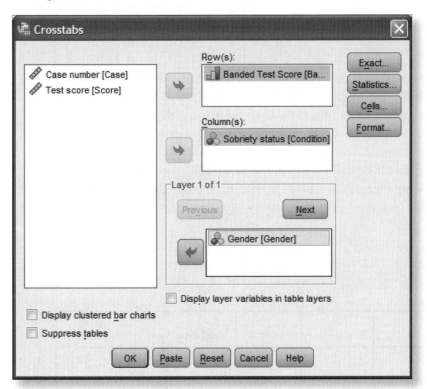

Variables with several values should be placed in rows to avoid wide printouts (the symbol by the banded variable denotes an ordinal measure). The other item of interest goes in the columns box. We have chosen to add Gender to the cross-tabulation as well. Again, there is a 'Next' button, but it should be noted that the more layers you have, the more difficult it is to analyse the 'Crosstabs' read-out.

Banded Test Score * Sobriety status * Gender Crosstabulation

Count

Gender			Sobriety status		Total
			sober	drinking	
Female	Banded Test Score	Low	2	1	3
		Medium	0	2	2
	Total		2	3	5
Male	Banded Test Score	Medium	2	2	4
		High	1	0	1
	Total		3	2	5

As will be noticed, even three variables make a relatively complicated cross-tabulation. It may be more informative to show a series of pairings, without layers.

If you just want the count for the individual variables, use *Analyze/Descriptive Statistics/Frequencies*. The banded test score, sobriety status and gender may all be asked for at once, but the output will be in frequency tables of individual variables:

Image 6.8

Banded Test Score

		Frequency	Percent	Valid Percent	Cumulative Percent
Valid	Low	3	30.0	30.0	30.0
	Medium	6	60.0	60.0	90.0
	High	1	10.0	10.0	100.0
	Total	10	100.0	100.0	

Similar boxes will appear for Sobriety status (split into 'sober' and 'drinking') and Gender ('female' and 'male').

Nominal data and contingency tables

Image 6.9

	Count	Agreement	Gender	var
1	1	1	1	
2	2	1	1	
3	3	1	2	
4	4	2	2	
5	5	2	2	
6	6	3	1	
7	7	3	1	
8	8	3	2	
9	9	3	2	
10	10	3	2	
11	11	3	2	
12	12	3	2	

Data View | Variable View

In this example, Variable View has already been set up: its Agreement 'Values' are set with the following labels: 1 = Yes, 2 = No, 3 = Don't know; the Gender labels are 1 = Female and 2 = Male. The 'Measures' for both variables have become Nominal. (While it is possible to adjust these variables to Type 'String' in order to input them as words such as 'Yes', we lose some functionality by doing so.) Remember to use a Count variable; it helps us to keep track of what we are doing when files are manipulated.

We can now read the statistics for each variable by using *Analyze/Descriptive Statistics/Frequencies*. Each variable receives its own frequency table. The frequencies can be used to produce pie charts on a spreadsheet; these are easier to set up and adjust than SPSS charts.

The Statistics option gives such statistics as the mean, median and mode.

However, to examine the relationship between these nominal variables, we need to create a contingency table. We use *Analyze/Descriptive Statistics/Crosstabs*

Image 6.10

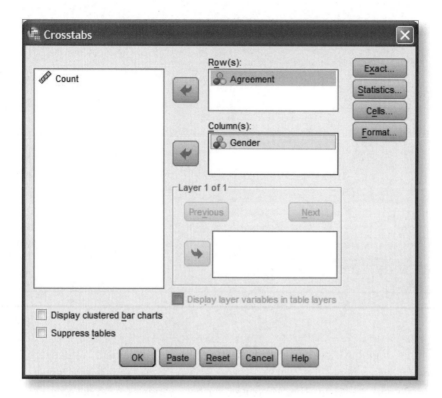

The variable with more options (3, as against 2 for gender) goes into 'Rows' to avoid too wide a read-out.

If we had more variables, the Layer box could be used to add another variable. When that is added, 'Next' can be used to add yet another. However, it should be noted that, while this may occasionally be useful, the more variables in the contingency table the less interpretable it may be.

The Statistics box is brought into action in the chapter on qualitative research (Chapter 8).

The case processing summary (not shown here) is worth checking in case of error. 'N' should equal the number of cases. The cross-tabulation will look like this:

Image 6.11

Agreement * Gender Crosstabulation

Count

		Gender		Total
		female	male	
Agreement	Yes	2	1	3
	No	0	2	2
	Don't know	2	5	7
Total		4	8	12

Summary data and contingency tables

There will be times when we will wish to add summaries of data (the frequencies) instead of raw data. For example, we may have found data from subsets and may wish to cross-tabulate them for statistical analysis.

Image 6.12

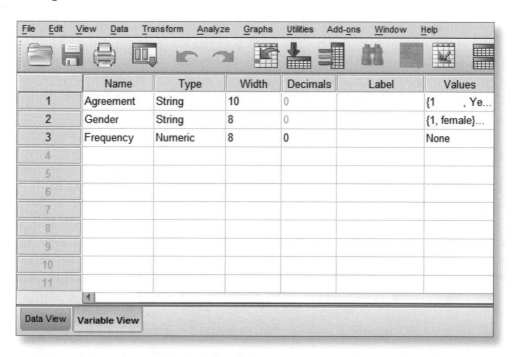

For this purpose, in Variable View, we need to create variables converted to Type 'String' to give them names. We give the Values labels as usual; the Agreement variable has been given a Width of 10 to hold 'don't know'. Most importantly, we have added a variable called Frequency and have given it zero decimals.

Image 6.13

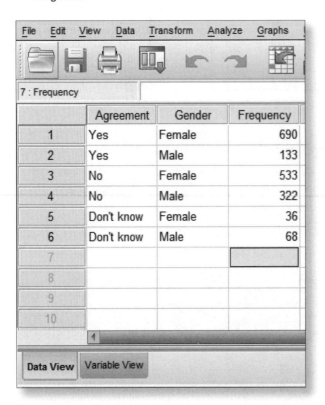

	Agreement	Gender	Frequency
1	Yes	Female	690
2	Yes	Male	133
3	No	Female	533
4	No	Male	322
5	Don't know	Female	36
6	Don't know	Male	68
7			
8			
9			
10			

We then enter the possible permutations in Data View, with the summary data under 'Frequency'. Follow this by using *Data/Weight Cases*. Select 'Weight cases by' and transfer 'Frequency'. Press 'OK'.

Image 6.14

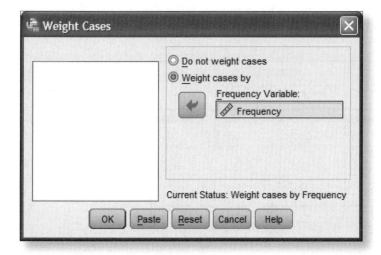

(Some writers use the word 'Count'. I prefer 'Frequency' to avoid confusion with the case numbers, which can lead to some very strange calculations indeed.)

Then use *Analyze/Descriptive Statistics/Crosstabs.*

Image 6.15

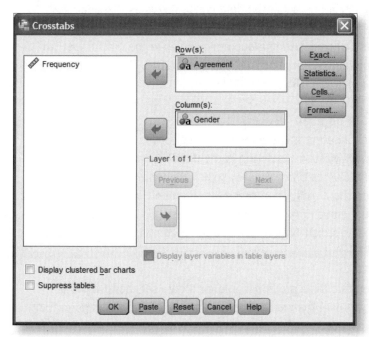

Image 6.16

Agreement * Gender Crosstabulation

Count

		Gender		Total
		Female	Male	
Agreement	Don't know	36	68	104
	No	533	322	855
	Yes	690	133	823
Total		1259	523	1782

At this stage the table does not look much more informative than the original input. However, with more complicated subsets and when it comes to the calculation of qualitative data, this becomes a very useful procedure.

Look at your data in closer detail

As will be seen at times in this book, the data is not always as it seems. For continuous and ordinal data, more statistics can be forthcoming from *Analyze/ Descriptive Statistics/Explore*. Putting grouping variables in the 'Factor List' will allow a breakdown of such information into category groups. You may also choose to use the 'Graphs' menu of SPSS.

Decide on the test to be used

This issue will be described in more detail in the rest of the book. However, one thing that is always worth considering is the distribution. To generate a distribution chart use *Graphs/Chart Builder*, select a simple histogram and put the relevant data into the X axis. Then press the 'Element Properties' button and select 'Display normal curve'; press 'Apply'. Then press 'OK' to see the output. As well as seeing your data's distribution, you can get a comparison with the normal distribution.

For deciding if parametric tests are applicable for a data set, however, it is recommended that you use *Analyze/Descriptive Statistics/Explore* and go to 'Plots', selecting 'Normality plots with tests'. The Shapiro–Wilk test is for data sets of less than 50; for larger numbers, read the Kolmogorov–Smirnov. If these tests are significant (for example Sig .000), they indicate that the data set does *not* have a normal distribution.

Record, expand and report

Decisions made, including the omission of data, should be recorded. Spreadsheet charts are widely considered to be more easily modifiable than those within SPSS. Means (or medians, in the case of non-parametric data) and relevant labels may be transferred to a spreadsheet such as Microsoft Excel for the creation of additional charts. So can cross-tabulations of frequencies. Remember to 'paste special' to a text format rather than into picture format.

It should be noted that, in the case of the transfer of raw scores onto a spreadsheet, data conversion would be needed. Between-subjects scores would need to be split up, with each grouping's data lined up beside each other in columns on the spreadsheet. This conversion can be undertaken in an automated way, as follows.

Select cases

SPSS provides various ways of examining data in greater detail. One method is **selecting cases**. Let us say that we wanted to examine gender by viewing males and females separately. In our 'Different' file males were given the code number 2. Go to the menu item Data/Select Cases. Select the 'If condition is satisfied' option, then the 'If' button.

Image 6.17

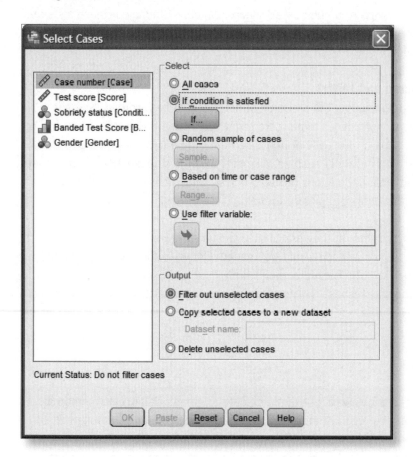

This leads to the 'Select Cases: If' dialog. Highlight 'Gender' on the left and press the arrow to enter it on the right. Then type = or click the = button (note: the ~= means 'not equal to') and then the number. So you would have Gender = 2.

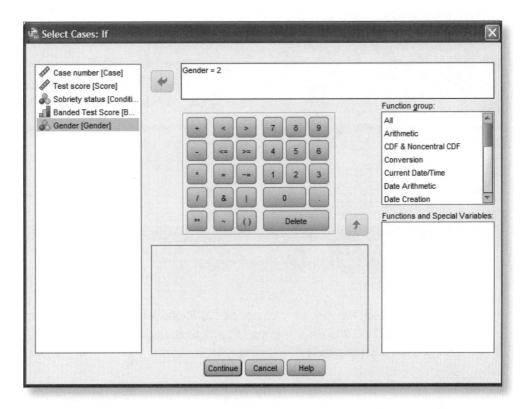

Pressing 'Continue' leads back to the 'Select Cases' dialog; follow by pressing 'OK'. The status bar at the bottom carries the reminder 'filter on' and diagonal lines will be found on some of the far left gray tabs of Data View; these are deselected cases. You will now find that any analysis of variables in the data set will only apply to the male cases.

Image 6.19

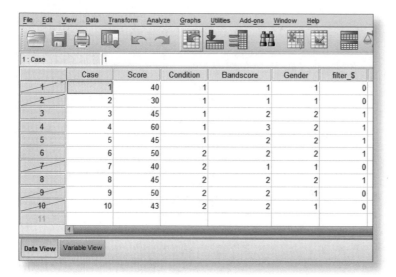

Do remember to check the status, which appears at the bottom right of the program (in this case, it will be 'Filter On'), in order to avoid recording a sub-sample when you think you are recording the entire data set, or vice-versa.

To cancel, go to Data/Select Cases. At the Select Cases dialog box, opt for 'All Cases' and click 'OK'.

Other data handling techniques

Another data handling technique in the Data part of the menu includes **Split Files**, which allows you to examine data sets by breaking up the measure of interest according to one or more grouping variables. (If you use this, do remember to 'reset' when you no longer want this to happen.)

Yet another is **Sort Cases**. This and other techniques can be looked up in the SPSS Help file or in the SPSS manuals (IBM, 2011).

Reporting of data

This is discussed in Chapter 13.

Talking point

As will become obvious later, it is important to examine data in a graphical format before getting carried away with the wildly significant (or depressingly insignificant) results of your statistical test.

Part Two
Statistical testing

Chapter 7
The analysis of differences

Deciding on the question

People thinking about everyday data may think of research design as a rather abstract concept. Design needs to be considered, however, every time we ponder which question should be asked (if any). The question of design must be posed before an appropriate test can be selected. It is presumed here, however, that we have already decided that we want to test for significant differences between data sets.

Unrelated versus related design

On each occasion, we need to look at the constituents of the sample.

In **unrelated design** different participants/records are used in each condition. If we are testing for differences between typing speeds on Mondays and Tuesdays, this would mean one group of staff being tested on a Monday, and another different group of people being tested on a Tuesday. Although this would get rid of order effects (for example, people getting bored with tests on the second occasion) or practice effects (getting better with practice), there is an obvious problem: any test is going to have to take into account a range of individual differences and is going to differ from a test applied to related designs.

Related design endeavours to get rid of these individual differences by one of two methods. The *same* people can be used in all conditions. In our typing example, the same people are tested on both Monday and Tuesday. This eliminates individual differences entirely, although not order/practice effects or the possibility of having a 'bad day'.

Another related design method is the **pairing** (or **matching**) of different participants for particular characteristics. In our typing example, although different people are tested on each day, each person's results are paired with the results of another person with, say, the same pre-tested typing speed, maybe also controlled for gender and seniority. This being the case, we eliminate practice/order effects while also eliminating some individual differences. In terms of testing, the paired or matched design is usually subsumed under the related design category.

Here are some alternative terms you may come across:

Table 7.1

Unrelated design	Related design
Different subjects/participants	Same subjects/participants
Between-subjects design	Within-subjects design
Unpaired	Paired
Unmatched	Matched
	Repeated measures (the same over time)
	Panel data (the same people over time, but this term is used in business statistics/econometrics)

Two or more conditions

Our discussion of Monday and Tuesday dealt with two conditions. In our typing example, however, we may wish to extend our analysis to every day of the week (giving five **conditions**). Another example could examine the differences between a range of different medical treatments (T1, T2, T3).

Data type

This chapter deals with measurable data, where, at the very least, each observation can be compared numerically. For nominal (categorical) data, see Chapter 8, which deals with qualitative analysis.

A note on research design terminology

In our typing example, by running a test, we are running an **experiment** (even if not strictly controlled under laboratory conditions). We are manipulating **variables**, types of phenomena which are changeable (variable). We are actively manipulating an independent variable. In the typing example, we are interested in the effect of the day of the week; it could be, however, the type of medical treatment, or a single treatment effect. We observe the effect of manipulating the **independent variable** by looking at changes in the **dependent variable**, that which is being measured. The independent variable is varied according to the will of the experimenter, independent of real life if you like, with the dependent variable being the data dependent on such variations. The terms independent variable and dependent variable should, strictly speaking, only be used in relation to experimental data but are widely used in other contexts.

Most 'real-world' analyses of differences between data sets are **quasi-experimental**. We do not manipulate variables ourselves but take them from records or from observations without planned allocation of participants into groups; and, if we choose to use pairing/matching (comparing people with similar relevant attributes), this would be done through taking details from records rather than actually selecting groups of people for an experiment. In a quasi-experimental version of our typing speeds study, the effect of the day of the week would be called a **predictor** (rather than an independent variable) and the typing speed would be the **criterion** (rather than the dependent variable). The criteria for measurement can be typing speeds, time of recovery from illness, number of relapses and so on.

Table 7.2

Dependent Variable/Criterion: Typing speed (in wpm)	Independent Variable/Predictor: Day of the week	
	Condition 1: Monday	Condition 2: Tuesday
	40	50
	30	40
	45	45
	60	50
	45	43

The terms predictor and criterion should be used in non-experimental research, although these are often interchangeable with independent and dependent variables in the literature. Both terms are used in the following example (ignore the results; we would, of course, want more than 5 records in each condition).

And now, to the tests!

Same subjects, two conditions

Wilcoxon – a non-parametric test

In this example, the same members of the public have filled in a 5-point scale describing their attitudes toward a local housing service and also toward a neighbouring service. Lower scores indicate hostility, higher scores approval. As this scale has not undergone preliminary calibration, a non-parametric test has been chosen. Being a small data set, we settled for a .05 level of significance; but as we did not know which service would be preferred, we opted for the more rigorous two-tailed hypothesis.

Table 7.3

		Predictor: Housing service	
		Condition 1: Ours	Condition 2: Theirs
Criterion: Attitude	person 1	4	5
	person 2	3	3
	person 3	2	4
	person 4	4	5
	person 5	3	5
	person 6	4	2
	person 7	3	3
	person 8	5	4
	person 9	3	5
	person 10	4	5
	person 11	3	5
	person 12	2	4
	person 13	2	5

Input process
Open SPSS and opt for 'Type in data'. Ensure that you are in Variable View.
Under Name in column 1, enter Case; in row 2, type Ours and in row 3, Theirs.

The Label cell for Case is expanded to 'Person number' (or 'Case number' if you prefer), Ours becomes 'Our service' and Theirs, 'Their service'. To get rid of trailing decimal points, it is recommended that you set all three Decimal settings to zero. As this is a same-subjects (or related) sample, we do not have a grouping variable and thus do not need 'Values' for transforming numbers.

Then, in Data View, enter the figures as given in the table above.

As noted in Chapter 5, you do not have to enter the case numbers manually. After entering the data as above, use *Transform/Compute Variable* and $casenum.

Save the file, perhaps with the name 'Services'.

Analysis

For non-parametric data we really want the median rather than the mean. This being the case, use *Analyze/Descriptive Statistics/Frequencies.*

Image 7.1

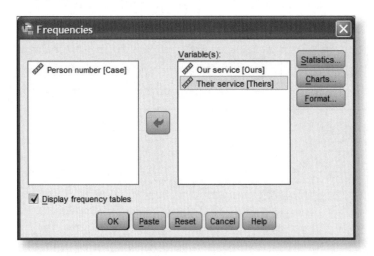

Use the 'Statistics' button to select the median (the mean and mode, and a sum of the totals are also available). To get a visual representation, use the 'Charts' button within the same procedure.

We see a considerable difference between the medians, 3 for 'ours' and 5 for 'theirs'.

The bar chart gives an effective picture of the differences between the two variables. (If you had opted for the histogram with a superimposed normal curve, you would have seen just how abnormal our data is and thus its unsuitability for a parametric test.)

We want to ascertain, however, that the more positive result for 'Theirs' is significant, so we use the Wilcoxon test. We can use *Analyze/Nonparametric Tests/Related Samples*. Use the 'Fields' tab at the top and transfer the measures (our service, their service) to the right of the dialog box.

Pressing the 'Run' button will show the Wilcoxon result as .036, rejecting the null hypothesis at a significance level of $p < .05$. If you select *Analyze/Nonparametric Tests/Legacy Dialogs/Two* Related Samples (the dialog box is in the following image) you will see that the .036 represents a two-tailed result. When we have reason to expect a one-tailed test of significance, the significance level can be halved, but in this case it would not be low enough to declare the next usually quoted figure, $p < .02$.

Image 7.2

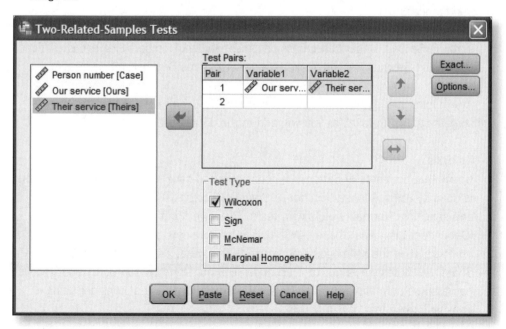

Paired T test (also known as related T test) – a parametric test

Students who didn't pass an examination initially, all achieving less than the 40 point pass mark, retook their examinations with generally improved results ('First'). They retook a second time ('Second') in an attempt to improve their grades further.

Table 7.4

		Predictor: Examination retakes	
		Condition 1: First	Condition 2: Second
Criterion: **Score**	person 1	52	60
	person 2	53	34
	person 3	47	38
	person 4	40	52
	person 5	48	54
	person 6	45	55
	person 7	52	36
	person 8	47	48
	person 9	51	44
	person 10	38	56

Input process

In Variable View, under Name in column 1, row 1, enter Case; in row 2, type First and in row 3, Second. Under Label, Case becomes 'Student Number', First becomes 'First retake' and Second, 'Second retake'. Again, set all three Decimal settings to zero.

After typing the figures into Data View, it may be useful to save the file as something like 'Retake', as you will add to the data shortly.

Analysis

Check that both sets of data can be considered to have a normal distribution. This is done by using *Analyze/Descriptive Statistics/Explore*, using the 'Plots' button and selecting 'Normality plots with tests'. Put both 'First' and 'Second' in the 'Dependent List'. The Shapiro–Wilk test is for data sets of up to 50; for larger numbers, read the Kolmogorov–Smirnov. In this case, we read the results of the Shapiro–Wilk test, p values of .225 and .365, not significant in both cases, so we can assume normality. (If the data is not normally distributed, consider using a non-parametric test, the Wilcoxon.)

Within the Explore procedure we see means of 47.3 and 47.7, but is this difference of .4 significant?

We now use *Analyze/Compare Means/Paired–Samples T Test*. Highlight 'First Retake' and 'Second Retake', using the arrow to move them to the Paired Variables window on the right. Press 'OK'.

The large *p* value (.922 two-tailed) tells us that the difference is not significant. The examination retake does not appear to have been a success.

Same subjects, more than two conditions

Friedman – a non-parametric test

This extends the Wilcoxon test. We use our 'Services' file from the Wilcoxon test exercise, adding a new condition. Our service, worried by the comparative success of the rival service, has attempted to improve its work (or maybe its image).

Table 7.5

		Predictor: Housing service		
		Condition 1: Ours	Condition 2: Theirs	Condition 3: Ours adapted
Criterion: Attitude	person 1	4	5	5
	person 2	3	3	3
	person 3	2	4	2
	person 4	4	5	2
	person 5	3	5	2
	person 6	4	2	2
	person 7	3	3	1
	person 8	5	4	3
	person 9	3	5	2
	person 10	4	5	4
	person 11	3	5	2
	person 12	2	4	3
	person 13	2	5	1

Input process

If you are restarting SPSS, opt for 'Open an existing data source'. In Variable View, write 'Adapted' in the next row under Name; again set Decimal to zero and under Label write 'Ours adapted'. In Data View, you will find a new 'Adapted' column in which you enter the data in Condition 3 above (the other columns are unchanged).

Analysis

To look at the basic statistics we use *Analyze/Descriptive Statistics/Frequencies* and press the 'Statistics' button to select the median statistic (although mean is also available). A glance indicates that this new-look service is perceived as being worse than its predecessor as well as worse than the neighbouring service.

Image 7.3

Statistics		Our service	Their service	Ours adapted
N	Valid	13	13	13
	Missing	0	0	0
Median		3.00	5.00	2.00

You can try *Analyze/Nonparametric Tests/Related Samples*, using the 'Fields' tab to transfer 'Our service', 'Their service' and 'Ours adapted' to the right-hand box and then press 'Run'. We see the Friedman p value as .002, with a significance of $p < .05$. Personally, I find that a little confusing. So let us look at *Analyze/ Nonparametric Tests/Legacy Dialogs/K Related Samples* (K just means any number above two). Ensure that the three variables are in the right-hand 'Test Variables' box and that the Friedman test has been selected and press 'OK'. Here, you are given the p value of .002. I would interpret that as $p < .01$.

There is a significant overall difference between the three conditions. Given that the new-look service is rated as much worse than the neighbouring service, it is clearly a case of back to the drawing board.

You may wish to follow up with significance tests of the pairs using the Wilcoxon test. However, the previous warning about dredging – increasing the number of possible false positives – means that we should multiply our significance levels. One way of adjusting for this is the Bonferroni method which requires a multiplication by the number of potential tests. If you run *Analyze/Nonparametric Tests/Legacy Dialogs/2 Related Samples*, you can run the test comparing the pairs.

Image 7.4

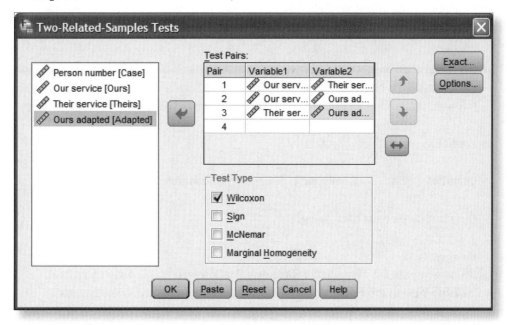

Image 7.5

	Test Statistics[c]		
	Their service - Our service	Ours adapted - Our service	Ours adapted - Their service
Z	-2.092[a]	-2.153[b]	-2.831[b]
Asymp. Sig. (2-tailed)	.036	.031	.005

a. Based on negative ranks.

b. Based on positive ranks.

c. Wilcoxon Signed Ranks Test

According to the Bonferroni method the *p* values (significance) should become 3 x .036, 3 x .031 and 3 x .005. These would give .108, .093 and .015 – only the last comparison, the largest difference, would be seen as significant, *p* < .02.

Some statisticians consider Bonferroni as rather severe (for example, Rice, 1989). I would venture to be a little softer: perhaps we could multiply by the number of pairings minus .5. So we multiply the significance values by 2.5: again, however, only the last of these would be seen as significant, giving .01, again p < .02.

Within-subjects one-way ANOVA – a parametric test (alternative: Friedman)

We use this analysis of variance, also called a repeated measures ANOVA, for more than two conditions, here working on an extended version of our 'Retakes' file (from the paired *t* test). Do note that this requires the SPSS Advanced Module. The alternative to this test is to use the previous test, the Friedman, the results of which are shown later.

Predictor: *Examination Retakes*

Condition 1: *First*   **Condition 2**: *Second*   **Condition 3:** *Third*

Our candidates have tried again.

Input process

Re-opening the file containing retake examination results, we enter 'Third' in Variable View in the next row in the same way as the previous two variables. In Data View, we then enter the following ten numbers alongside the other two columns of data: 62, 56, 40, 37, 62, 56, 68, 55, 68, 60.

Analysis

First we look at the descriptive data. *You should always do EDA (exploratory data analysis) before running an ANOVA.* We need to check the assumptions of normal distribution and that the data is suitably measurable.

One option for parametric data is to use *Analyze/Descriptive Statistics/Descriptives.* However, we can get more information from *Analyze/Descriptive Statistics/Explore.* Put the three conditions into the Dependent Variables box, press the 'Plots' button to select 'Normality plots with tests' and then 'OK'.

The Shapiro–Wilk test, which we use for conditions with less than 50 cases, is not significant (Kolmogorov–Smirnov is for 50 or more). So, there is no indication of abnormality in the new column of data. A parametric test may be used. Having said that, the Box plot indicates two outliers in the new set of cases. You would need to check that cases 3 and 4 are legitimate data as opposed to input errors.

Image 7.6

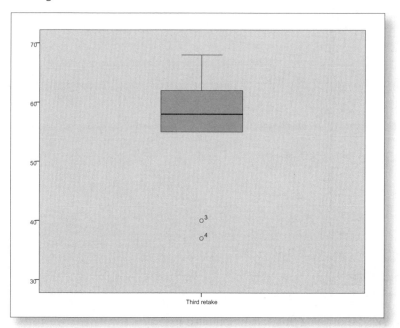

(Some notes about box and whisker plots: the box represents 50% of the data in the variable. The thick line in the middle of the box is the median. On either side of the median are the upper and lower quartiles, each representing 25% of the data. Most of the data is typically held within whiskers above and below the box. Here, however, there is no low score whisker. We only see points – '3' and '4' – which are outliers.)

As we have parametric data, we decide to use the one-way analysis of variance rather than the Friedman test. We choose *Analyze/General Linear Model/ Repeated Measures* (do note, you want 'General Linear *Model*', singular, not the 'General Linear *Models*' menu option). In the Repeated Measures Define Factor(s) dialog box, replace 'factor1' with your own chosen factor name (here, 'retake'). Note that all names in this dialog box must be eight or fewer characters and start with a lower case letter. Then put the number 3 into the 'Number of Levels'.

Image 7.7

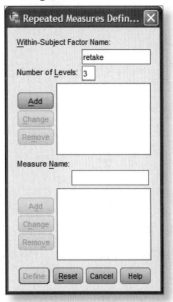

After pressing 'Add', the dialog box should look like this:

Image 7.8

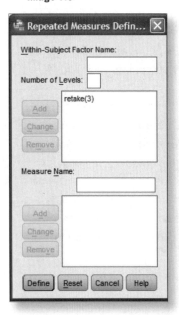

Then put a dependent variable name in the 'Measure Name' box, here 'score'.

Image 7.9

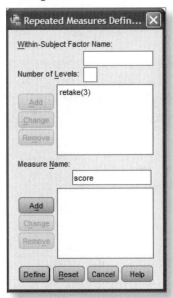

Then press 'Add'. You should then see the following image (I am putting a fair amount of detail into preparing repeated measures tests, as people have been known to have trouble getting this procedure to work.)

Image 7.10

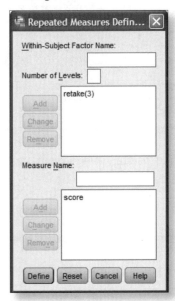

Then click 'Define' to go to the Repeated Measures dialog box. Transfer the variables First, Second and Third to the right, replacing the default question marks shown in the next picture.

Image 7.11

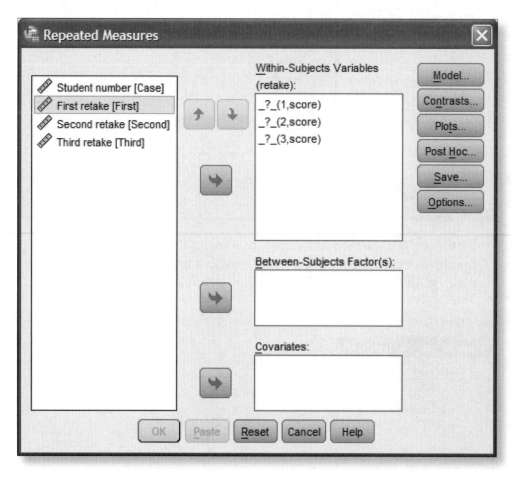

(ANOVA can become more complicated, especially when we start to analyse more than one factor, so it is worth getting into the habit of doing this one by one to avoid errors.) The finished box should look like this:

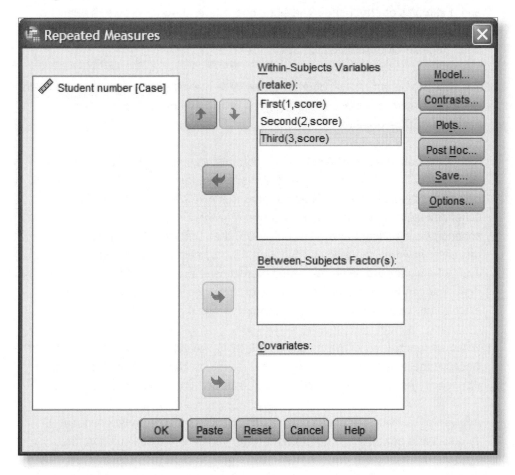

We don't need the 'Between-subjects' box until we reach the chapter on factorial ANOVA (Chapter 10) and more specifically the mixed design ANOVA (where we combine within– and between-subjects factors).

The Covariates box is for variables which do not interest us in particular but which we consider may have an influence on interactions. This would allow the software to control for this extraneous factor in an analysis of covariance (ANCOVA). (Covariance and ANCOVA are discussed towards the end of Chapter 10). As this is a controversial procedure, you should definitely read about it before even thinking about using it.

Go to the Options box, transfer 'retake' to the 'Display Means for' box on the right. Select the 'Compare main effects' tick box and set the 'Confidence interval adjustment' to 'Sidak' (to be discussed shortly). Also tick 'Descriptive statistics' and 'Estimates of effect size'. The significance level box at the bottom relates to analysis of the pairs of conditions (levels). Press 'Continue' and then 'OK' in the main Repeated Measures dialog box.

The first two output boxes confirm that we have the data input correct and provide the basic statistics. (In academic reporting, it is common to cite the standard deviation, 'SD', as well as the mean.)

Ignore the output on multivariate tests, both at this stage and later in the readout. You will then see Mauchly's Test of Sphericity. In addition to the assumptions for parametric tests in general, repeated measures ANOVAs have an assumption of sphericity (equality of the variances between each pair of levels). If the test of sphericity is significant at the level of $< .05$, then the assumption is violated. In this case, however, the reading ('Sig.') of .432 is healthily non-significant. In the event of a significant result, we would then consult the 'Epsilon' figures to the right. You can find a detailed discussion of this when the problem arises in the exercise on two-way ANOVA mixed design, towards the end of Chapter 10.

When we reach Tests of Within-subjects Effects, we get to the heart of the matter. Because the sphericity test was non-significant, you can read from the top row ('Sphericity Assumed'): $F = 3.706$ Sig. $= .045$ and Partial Eta Squared $= .292$

Analysis of variance calculates how much variance comes from independent variables and how much is due to error (error variance). The calculation, the variance divided by the error, is the F ratio, referred to in the output as 'F'. This is discussed in more detail in the discussion of statistical theory near the end of the chapter on factorial analysis (Chapter 10). Essentially, the bigger the F ratio, the more likely it is that the effect is a significant one.

So we have a critical value of $p < .05$ – our effect is a significant one. We can reject the null hypothesis that the variances are equal.

If the sphericity test proved to be significant, then we would read off one of the rows referred to as Greenhouse–Geisser or Huyn–Feldt. Please consult the exercise on mixed ANOVA (Chapter 10) for some guidance on this.

Partial Eta Squared refers to the effect size, in this case a small one.

Effect size and the analysis of differences

One rule of thumb is that an effect size of 0.2 to 0.5 is small, 0.5 to 0.8 is medium and greater than 0.8 is large.

Ignore the 'Within-subjects contrasts' output.

Image 7.13

Pairwise Comparisons

Measure: score

(I) retake	(J) retake	Mean Difference (I-J)	Std. Error	Sig.[b]	95% Confidence Interval for Difference[b]	
					Lower Bound	Upper Bound
1	2	-.400	3.964	1.000	-11.987	11.187
	3	-9.100*	2.885	.035	-17.531	-.669
2	1	.400	3.964	1.000	-11.187	11.987
	3	-8.700	4.333	.210	-21.366	3.966
3	1	9.100*	2.885	.035	.669	17.531
	2	8.700	4.333	.210	-3.966	21.366

Based on estimated marginal means
* The mean difference is significant at the .05 level.
b. Adjustement for multiple comparisons: Sidak.

If we consult the Pairwise Comparisons table, we find that the difference between the means of retake 1 and retake 3 is denoted by an asterisk as significant (if we had adjusted our significance expectation to < .01 then this would no longer be the case). Our p value of .035 is smaller than the critical value of $p < .05$.

The confidence intervals refer, at a 95% estimate, to how broad the ranges of values are likely to be. This concept is probably more useful for qualifying predictions from rather larger data sets. Let us move away from this and briefly consider the nature of the multiple comparison tests.

To counteract the possibility of fluke results creating false positives, an adjustment is often made in the case of multiple comparisons of pairs. We have used the Sidak test. The alternative test, Bonferroni, is these days considered by some to be overly harsh (Rice, 1989). However, if you try the Bonferroni in this case, the p value is the same for our significant result and only slightly increased for the relationship between retakes 3 and 2. In many cases, both tests will give similar results. The choice of comparison tests is discussed at greater length in the statistical theory box near the end of the chapter on factorial analysis (Chapter 10).

If you had used the default LSD setting, basically without the adjustments in place to avoid statistical flukes, you would still only find one significant result, although at a critical value of $p < .02$. However, while the relationship between retake 3 and retake 2 is still non-significant, we could refer to the p value of .076 as a *trend* towards significance. While the statistical adjustments are designed to stop false positives (Type 1 errors), it is quite possible that our rather small data set has led us to a Type 2 error, a false negative.

Here I have consulted the LSD result as an exercise. Usually we would have to have theoretical backing for using this, a clear expectation that the not quite significant result should have been so. As we have no clear reason for retake 3 making a substantial difference, looking at the LSD result in this situation would be dredging (a no–no, as you know).

The Friedman alternative

If you do not have access to the repeated measures ANOVA, similar results emerge from using the previous test, the Friedman. The result here is .025, giving the same standard critical value of $p < .05$.

In the absence of the comparison tests offered by ANOVA, we also have the possibility of running sets of paired t tests to examine relationships between individual pairs of data. Do remember, however, that as you were advised at the end of the main discussion of the Friedman test, these post hoc tests should have their significance adjusted somewhat.

Use *Analyze/Compare Means/Paired–Samples T Test*, putting all three pairings in the right-hand box. We get the same results as in the LSD pairing comparisons. If we use my crude Bonferroni technique and multiply the .012 p value for retakes 1 and 3 (.012 *3 = .036), we get something very close to the Bonferroni output for the ANOVA. If we use my milder method and reduce the pairing number by .5 (.012 *2 .5 = .03), the significance is still $p < .05$.

Our results suggest that something has happened in terms of the examination results, but it is unclear precisely what. Perhaps another effect is in play. We were warned by the box plot that the third set of data was peculiar.

Different subjects, two conditions

Mann–Whitney – a non-parametric test

A chain of estate agents regularly receives complaints about the endowment policies it recommends for the paying-off of mortgages. It is now examining the effects of different types of warning notice upon the level of complaints made about each office. Some offices have a wall-poster describing the situations in which endowments are appropriate for mortgages; others pass their clients leaflets as part of a sales pack.

Table 7.6

	Predictor: Warning method			
	Condition 1: Wall-poster		Condition 2: Leaflet	
Criterion: Number of complaints (per branch)	office 1	5	office 11	6
	office 2	4	office 12	15
	office 3	16	office 13	4
	office 4	6	office 14	4
	office 5	7	office 15	6
	office 6	22	office 16	7
	office 7	8	office 17	16
	office 8	9	office 18	7
	office 9	9	office 19	5
	office 10	8	office 20	4

Input process

The table above is produced as you would use it in Excel. However, *between-subjects data sets are entered differently in SPSS*, as in the following table:

Table 7.7

1	5	1
2	4	1
3	16	1
4	6	1
5	7	1
6	22	1
7	8	1
8	9	1
9	9	1
10	8	1
11	6	2
12	15	2
13	4	2
14	4	2
15	6	2
16	7	2
17	16	2
18	7	2
19	5	2
20	4	2

The case number is on the left, the scores are in the centre and the two conditions are distinguished by grouping variables (1 and 2).

Using the Data Editor's Variable View, on row number 1, put the Name as 'Case', on row 2 as 'Score' and on Row 3 'Method'. In each case, set Decimals to zero. In the Label column, rename Case as 'Office Number', Score as 'Number of Complaints' and Method as 'Warning Type'. For the Method row, in order to make our Warning Types meaningful, go to the Value column and give names to the grouping variables. So you click the dotted area to the right of the cell. In the dialog box, add 1 to the *value* field in the dialog box and 'poster' in the *label* field, then press *add*. Then do likewise for 2 and 'leaflet'. These labels will appear in the output instead of the numbers. The Method row should also be altered in the Measure column to Nominal (we are unlikely to want to allocate ranks to these categories).

Do the same with 2 and the word 'leaflet'. These will become value labels. So when you write 1 or 2 in Data View, these are replaced by 'poster' and 'leaflet' respectively. Press 'OK'.

Then enter your data in Data View and save the file (something like 'Mortgage').

Analysis

First we check for the normality of our data, in case we want to use a parametric test. We use *Analyze/Descriptive Statistics/Explore*, using the 'Plots' button to select 'Normality plots with tests'. Put the measure in the 'Dependent List' and the grouping variable into the 'Factor List'. Press 'OK'.

Image 7.14

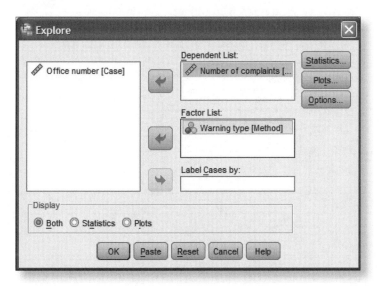

In each condition, we are told by a significant Shapiro–Wilk test that the sample is unlikely to be from a normal distribution (we would read the Kolmogorov–Smirnov for 50 or more cases), so we should be using a non-parametric test. You will also note, by the way, that the box plots show outliers – these really throw parametric tests.

We then look at the descriptive data – *Analyze/Descriptive Statistics/Explore*, where with nonparametric data, we are particularly interested in the medians. Unlike means, these are not sensitive to the outliers. We see medians of 8 and 6.

To see if the differences between the medians are significant we use the Mann–Whitney test. Use *Analyze/Nonparametric Tests/Independent Samples*. Using the 'Fields' tab at the top, put the measure (number of complaints) into 'Test Fields' and the grouping variable (warning type) into 'Groups'. Press 'Run'.

We see a large significance value (.158) which indicates that there is no significant difference between the data sets and, therefore, no significant difference between the use of wall-posters and of leaflets in this scenario. It is suggested that you save this data set (for example 'Mortgage'), as the data will be added to later.

Unpaired T test (also known as independent T test) – a parametric test

In research into the effects of different office conditions, one group of office workers is given a lengthy proofreading task to do within enclosed offices; the other group does the same task in an open plan office.

Table 7.8

	Predictor: Office conditions		
		Score	Enclosed vs open plan
Criterion:	person 1	80	1
Task score	person 2	68	1
	person 3	77	1
	person 4	78	1
	person 5	85	1
	person 6	82	1
	person 7	79	1
	person 8	76	1
	person 9	77	1
	person 10	83	1
	person 11	84	1
	person 12	82	1
	person 13	81	1
	person 14	80	1
	person 15	56	2
	person 16	69	2
	person 17	73	2

Predictor: Office conditions			
		Score	Enclosed vs open plan
Criterion: Task score	person 18	70	2
	person 19	61	2
	person 20	65	2
	person 21	59	2
	person 22	60	2
	person 23	53	2
	person 24	61	2
	person 25	62	2
	person 26	71	2

Input process

In Excel, we would have had two columns, with the scores for cases 1 to 13 and the scores for 14 to 26. In SPSS, they share the same column but are separated by the grouping variable (here, '1' and '2').

(Notice that in this study, there are different numbers of participants in the different conditions; only 'same subject' studies are required to have the same numbers.)

Using the Data Editor's Variable View, on row number 1, put the Name as Case, on row 2 as Score and on row 3 Room. In each case, set Decimals to zero. In the Label column, rename Case as 'Person Number', Score as 'Task Score' and Room as 'Room Type'. In order to make our room types meaningful, go to the Room row's Value column and give names to grouping variables 1 and 2, for example, 'own office' and 'open plan'. These names will be shown during any output. The variable Room should be adjusted to 'Nominal' in the Measure column.

Then enter in Data View as usual. It is recommended that you 'save as' at some point during data entry (perhaps save as 'Office') and save regularly during input.

Analysis

We wish to ensure that a parametric test is appropriate, by checking for normality (as illustrated in the preceding Mann–Whitney exercise). Use *Analyze/Descriptive Statistics/Explore*, pressing the 'Plots' button to select 'Normality plots with tests'. The measure (score) is put in the 'Dependent List' and the grouping variable (room type) into the 'Factor List'. Press 'OK'.

Both sets of data appear to be normal, according to the non-significant Shapiro–Wilk test result (use Kolmogorov–Shapiro for data sets of 50 or more), so we can use a parametric test.

Use *Analyze/Compare Means/Independent–Samples T Test*. Put the score in the upper right-hand box as usual. However, when you place the grouping variable in its box, you will see the following:

Image 7.15

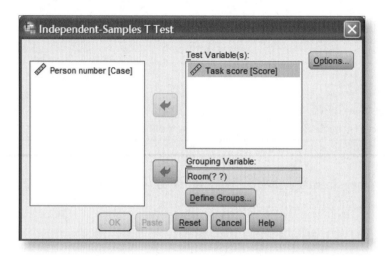

We are required to enter the values we use for the groups, here 1 and 2. Press 'Define Groups'.

Image 7.16

Then enter the two values for the grouping variable. After 'Continue', press 'OK' on the main dialog box to run the test.

If your two sets of data are of different sizes, as in this case, homogeneity of variance is necessary. The Levene test, which is integral to the read-out, examines this precondition. As with the normality tests, the Levene test needs to be *non–significant* in order to demonstrate homogeneity.

If the Levene test is significant, with a *p* value of .05 or less, then we would need to either return to the non-parametric equivalent, the Mann–Whitney test, or to ensure that the two data sets include the same number of cases. The second option is questionable methodologically: can you remove data without affecting the likely outcome, or can you be sure when adding data that the data is consistent?

In this case the Levene test read-out shows the significance level as .08, not significant, so we can continue using our parametric test with different data subsets.

We can see from the group statistics read-out that the mean scores for the 'own office' and 'open plan' conditions are 79.43 and 63.33 respectively. The *t* test shows that such a difference between the test scores is highly significant, less than .001 two-tailed. According to this (fictional) data, being in an open plan office seriously impairs performance on a proofreading task. Please keep this file ('Office') as it will be extended for another test.

Different subjects, more than two conditions

Kruskal–Wallis – a non– parametric test
Open the file with data on mortgages, previously used with the Mann–Whitney. We now have complaints data following the use of yet another method of warning, incorporating the necessary warnings into the sales talk.

We now want to add a third condition in this between-subjects design. The Kruskal–Wallis test can be considered an extension of the Mann–Whitney test.

Input process
In Variable View, find the Method/Warning Type row and go to the cell in the Value column, clicking the dotted area to the right of the cell. On the dialog

box, add 3 to the 'value' field in the dialog box and 'sales' in the 'label' field, then pressing 'Add'. After adding the third grouping variable to the box, press 'OK'. This ensures that the output will read 'sales' rather than the less than comprehensible '3'.

Image 7.17

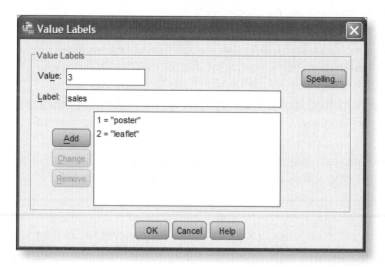

Then in Data View, add the following data to the Score column: 8, 4, 3, 12, 4, 4, 9, 8, 32, 6. Alongside the new scores, add the running numbers 21 to 30 in the Case/Office Number column and the number 3 in the Method/Warning Type column, which is a grouping variable with nominal measurement data. Remember to save the file.

Analysis

First check for normal distribution if you would prefer a parametric test. Use *Analyze/Descriptive Statistics/Explore,* using the 'Plots' button to select 'Normality plots with tests'. The measure is put in the 'Dependent List' and the grouping variable into the 'Factor List'. In this case, Shapiro–Wilk (Kolmogorov–Smirnov is for 50 or more cases) is significant ($p < .05$), so we cannot assume normality (also, check out the outliers on the box and whiskers plot). So we should use a non-parametric test.

Before moving away from the *Explore* read-out, we may extract the medians for report, 8, 6 and 7 for the poster, leaflet and sales methods respectively.

However, a quicker way of looking at the most basic statistics, especially if we want to copy data, is to use Analyze/Compare Means/Means. You do need to press the 'Options' button to add the medians to the read-out.

Image 7.18

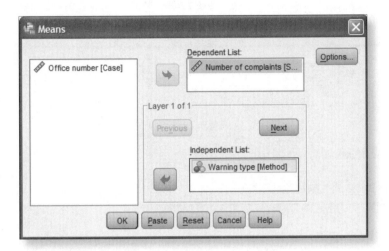

This gives a clear output of the basic statistics for each warning type, the medians being poster 8, leaflet 6 and sales 7.

To see if these results are significantly different, we use *Analyze/Nonparametric Tests/Independent Samples*. Use the 'fields' tab at the top, transferring the measure (complaints) to the 'Test Fields' box on the right and the grouping variable (warning type) in the 'Groups' slot.

After you press 'Run', you will find that the output refers to the Kruskal–Wallis test. The large *p* value of .409 indicates an insignificant result. There is no overall significant difference between warning methods.

It is possible to test individual pairings although the usual warning stands: hunting for tenuous results is likely to multiply (or inflate, if you like) the probability of chance results. You would use the Mann–Whitney test. If you run *Analyze/ Nonparametric Tests/Legacy Dialogs/2* Independent Samples, you can compare the different subsets.

Image 7.19

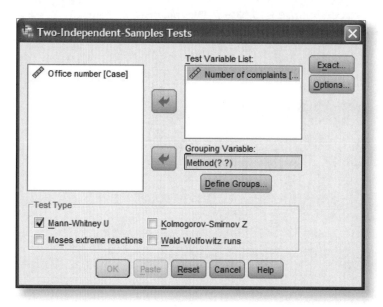

Image 7.20

When you press the 'Define Groups' button, you enter the relevant values, for example, 1 and 3 for 'poster' and 'sales', and then press 'Continue' and then 'OK'.

However, the previous warning about dredging – increasing the number of possible false positives – means that we should multiply our significance levels. The Bonferroni method requires a multiplication by 3 of the number of potential tests. If, in a hypothetical case, we have three subsets with the significance level of one particular pairing being .021 then, because there are three possible pairings, we have 3 * .021 = .063, which is not significant. However, as some statisticians consider Bonferroni unnecessarily harsh (for example, Rice, 1989), I suggest multiplying by the number of pairings minus .5 So we multiply the significance values by 2.5: this method still suggests that the result is not quite significant at $p < .05$ (2.5 x .021 = .0525).

Between-subjects one-way ANOVA – a parametric test

Although there is a clear productivity advantage in everybody having their own offices, this is expensive. If we were to introduce cubicles to break up the open plan office, would this produce better results than open plan?

Input process

Open the file about office conditions (unpaired *t* test). Using the Data Editor's Variable View, find the Method/Room Type row and go to the Value column, clicking the dotted area to the right of the cell. In the dialog box, add 3 to the value field and 'cubicle' in the label field, then pressing 'Add'. So in the output, 3 is replaced by 'cubicle'.

Then go to Data View and add the following 16 numbers at the bottom of the Score/Task Score column: 70, 70, 73, 80, 81, 75, 75, 73, 81, 76, 75, 75, 73, 71, 72, 67.

Add the running numbers 27 to 42 in the Case/Person Number column and the number 3 in the Method/Room Type column. Remember to save the file. (On larger data inputs, you should save regularly.)

Analysis

As usual we look at the descriptive data. *You should always do EDA (exploratory data analysis) before running an ANOVA.* We need to check the assumptions of normal distribution and that the data is suitably measurable. If you have chosen equal numbers for each group, you do not need to be concerned with the third assumption, homogeneity of variance; this issue will be discussed shortly when we get a read-out from the Levene test.

As usual, check for the normality of the data, to ensure that a parametric test is appropriate. Use *Analyze/Descriptive Statistics/Explore*, using the 'Plots' button to select 'Normality plots with tests'. The measure is put in the 'Dependent List' and the grouping variable into the 'Factor List'. Press 'OK'.

In this case, the Shapiro–Wilk test has a non-significant result, so there is no reason to assume non-normality. We can continue (Kolmogorov–Smirnov would have been used had there been 50 or more cases).

We can see a basic data read-out using *Analyze/Compare Means/Means*, which is described in more detail within the previous, Kruskal–Wallis, example. In this case, we have the following means: own office 79.4, open plan 63.3 and cubicle 74.2.

While having your own office was always going to lead to a speedier performance than open plan (assuming self-discipline), it appears that the cubicle system is also efficacious. However, we do not know yet whether or not the cubicle produces significantly better results than open plan. Also, we do not know if having your own office remains significantly productive compared to the new cubicle system. (Do remember, before planning a new office system, that this is a fictional data set.)

To examine significance, we use *Analyze/General Linear Model/Univariate*. (We could use *Analyze/Compare Means/One-Way ANOVA*, but this does not provide the Partial Eta Squared effect size statistic.)

Image 7.21

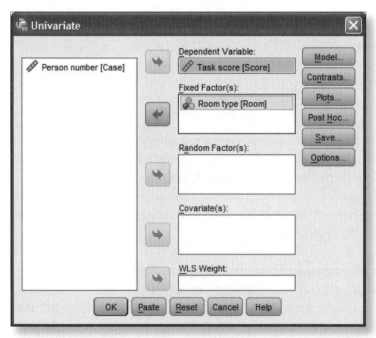

The Covariate box is for other variables which may influence interactions. Although ANCOVA (analysis of covariance) can control for extraneous factors, there are various assumptions to be met and I have considerable misgivings about using this procedure (see the end of Chapter 10). The Random Factors(s) box is also a rather advanced procedure and one which I think we should avoid.

Press the 'Post Hoc' button, move the relevant grouping category (room) into the box on the right and select 'Tukey'; this test allows us to examine the relationship between individual pairings. Press 'Continue'.

The 'Options' button allows us to select 'Homogeneity tests', which we need *if we have uneven numbers*. In such a case, the Levene Statistic needs to be non-significant. The Partial Eta Squared effect size statistic will also be needed if our main effect is significant. If we wish to, we can also adjust the significance level from its default of .05.

Image 7.22

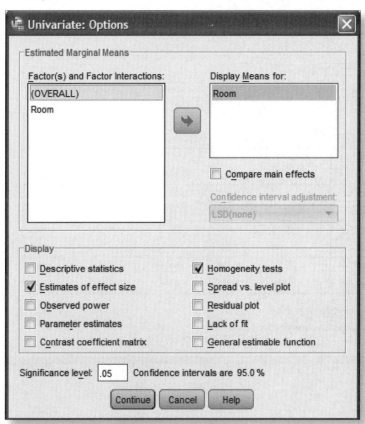

If the Levene test is significant, with a p value of .05 or less, then we would need to either return to the non-parametric equivalent, the Kruskal–Wallis test, or to ensure that the data sets include the same number of cases. The second option is questionable methodologically: can you remove the data without affecting the likely outcome, or can you be sure when adding new data that the data is consistent?

However, in our example, the Levene test is not significant (.089) so we can assume homogeneity of variance and may continue examining the results of the ANOVA.

When we look at the 'Tests of Between-subjects Effects' output table, we can ignore the 'Corrected Model' and 'Intercept' rows. We are really interested in 'Room', the main effect, which has an F ratio of 36.863, Sig. = .000, Partial Eta Squared .654 This is a highly significant result for the overall differences between the conditions, $p < .0005$ Partial Eta Squared is the estimated effect size, .654, indicating a medium sized effect. The 'Error' calculation you will see in the table refers to within-group variance.

The Multiple Comparisons output table shows the 'post hoc' examinations of the relationships between each pair of variables, using the Tukey test.

Image 7.23

					95% Confidence Interval	
(I) Room type	(J) Room type	Mean Difference (I-J)	Std. Error	Sig.	Lower Bound	Upper Bound
own office	open plan	16.10*	1.901	.000	11.46	20.73
	cubicle	5.24*	1.768	.014	.93	9.55
open plan	own office	-16.10*	1.901	.000	-20.73	-11.46
	cubicle	-10.85*	1.845	.000	-15.35	-6.36
cubicle	own office	-5.24*	1.768	.014	-9.55	-.93
	open plan	10.85*	1.845	.000	6.36	15.35

Task score
Tukey HSD

Based on observed means.
The error term is Mean Square(Error) = 23.347.

*. The mean difference is significant at the 0.05 level.

The three data rows allow us to look at the comparisons from the viewpoint of the three different conditions. The means for each condition are subtracted from each other in the Mean Difference column. The asterisks next to the data refer to significance; if the 'Options' significance setting had been set to .01, then not all of these would be asterisked, as we see when we look at the significance column. The differences between own office and open plan, and cubicle and open plan are significant at the level of $p < .0005$, whereas the difference between own office and cubicle is significant to only $p < .02$ The Confidence Intervals show that 95% of the time, we can be sure that the Mean Difference will be within these upper and lower limits; if we had set 'Options' to .01, then the Confidence Interval would be 99%.

Image 7.24

The

Task score

Tukey HSD[a,b,c]

Room type	N	Subset		
		1	2	3
open plan	12	63.33		
cubicle	16		74.19	
own office	14			79.43
Sig.		1.000	1.000	1.000

Means for groups in homogeneous subsets are displayed.

Based on observed means.

The error term is Mean Square(Error) = 23.347

    a. Uses Harmonic Mean Sample Size = 13.808

    b. The group sizes are unequal. The harmonic mean of the group sizes is used. Type 1 error levels are not guaranteed.

    C. Alpha = 0.5.

Homogeneous Subsets chart is another way of seeing which groups are significantly different from each other. In this case, the means from each condition sit in different columns, indicating that they are all significantly different from each other. In the event of a column containing more than one statistic, the conditions within the column would be not be significantly different from each other. This table is probably more useful when examining numerous variables.

It looks like Cubicles is a sensible compromise between the two other office layouts.

Clearly, however, if you can get your own office, it looks like a good idea.

Talking point

It is a commonplace truism that correlations (Chapter 9) do not prove 'cause and effect'. It can be argued that this can also be said of quasi-experimental structures.

Let us say that we replicate the examination retake study and it becomes increasingly clear that the third retake is a clear improvement on both of its predecessors. Would the students' improved performance stem from extended revision, more practice in taking examinations, or the fear of having to sit a fourth examination?

What we do not have is validity, that the results mean what we think they mean. To get more insights into a phenomenon, triangulation is always wise, running a rather different investigation in order to view the phenomenon from a fresh angle. New insights are often derived from this new perspective, sometimes leading to a complete rethink. In the case of our retake students, we could interview the students about their preparation, look at completion speeds and maybe also ask them about what they feel about the whole process. The last of these suggestions brings us to the topic of the next chapter, qualitative analysis.

This table of tests of difference is not exhaustive, but aims to provide a general guide.

N.B. Non-parametric tests can be used with 'parametric' data.

Table 7.9

Design	Test	Conditions	Data
Same or paired subjects	Wilcoxon	2	Non-parametric
	Paired *t* test	2	Parametric
	Friedman	3 or more	Non-parametric
	Within Subjects one-way ANOVA	3 or more	Parametric
Different subjects	Mann–Whitney	2	Non-parametric
	Unpaired *t* test	2	Parametric
	Kruskal–Wallis	3 or more	Non-parametric
	Between Subjects one-way ANOVA	3 or more	Parametric
Diagnostic tests for normal distribution	Shapiro–Wilk Kolmogorov–Smirnov	Less than 50 cases Larger numbers	Any data, to see if suitable for parametric tests

Chapter 8
Qualitative analysis

There will be many occasions on which you will have gathered a lot of information which does not appear to be quantifiable. People hold different impressions of a government policy; consumers fall into different 'types' of buyers or social class; different categories of situation or behaviour emerge from incident records. The data is *nominal*: such phenomena may not be assigned numerical values, as membership of one such *category* is not necessarily 'better' or weightier than another. We can count the *frequency* of their occurrence, however.

Data must be both *exclusive* and *exhaustive*: each observation can only be allocated to one category of the analysis and all observations from a sample must be allocated.

The statistical analyses here are concerned with comparing what is observed with what may be predicted. If our predictions are founded on chance, what may happen at random, then we are interested in whether or not actual observations differ significantly from predicted observations.

Statistical theory – come on, you know you like it!

Chi square and other qualitative methods
Numerically, we are interested here in 'frequencies', the number of times a case appears. The researcher devises a set of categories and gives a frequency to each category.

The statistical calculations contrast the 'observed frequencies' with the 'expected frequencies'. The observed frequencies are the actual results, or 'observations'. The expected frequencies are those which would be anticipated if the results were due to chance. The null hypothesis can be rejected if the statistical test being used indicates a significant difference between the observed and expected frequencies.

This general treatment of predictions based on chance has implications for our use of *p* values. Generally, a two-tailed *p* value is the correct choice. You should only use a one-tailed result if there is a weighty theoretical reason for one option to be predictably superior (not just 'I always felt that was the better one').

Dichotomies – the binomial test

Let us select a case of a simple 'heads or tails' (dichotomous) event. People walk through a park and they can choose to fork left around a clump of trees or they can fork right around the same clump. Assume that the view is pretty much the same in either direction and that the clump looks rather uninviting. If we observe 30 individuals and find that 17 go left and 13 go right, it is likely that any statistical test is likely to find the difference between the observed 17:13 and the predicted 15:15 to be insignificant.

It should be noted that the probability of one condition or the other – success or failure, if you like – must remain the same throughout: 50:50.

Input process

For direct data entry (usually for small samples)
Go to Variable View and name one variable, for example, 'tree'. The Measure field should be adjusted to 'Nominal' and Decimal to '0'. When you get to the Value column, click the dotted area to the right of the cell. On the Value Labels dialog box, place 1 in the value field and 'left' in the label field, then press 'Add'. Do the same with 2 and the word 'right'. Press 'OK'.

Then enter the data (only using the chosen values – here, 1 and 2) on one column of Data View.

	tree	
1	1	
2	2	
3	1	
4	2	
5	2	
6	2	
7	2	
8	1	
9	2	
10	2	
11	1	
12	2	

Data View | Variable View

Select *Analyze/Nonparametric Tests/Legacy Dialogs/Binomial* (this is simpler than the *Analyze/Nonparametric Tests/One Sample*, but both do the same job). Transfer the variable 'tree' to the Test Variable List. *Leave the small 'Test Proportion' box at 0.50 (that is, 50:50).* Click 'OK' and you will start to get the results of the test (here, non-significant).

To enter summary data instead of raw data

When you are dealing with larger amounts of data, or data in subsets, it will probably be easier to enter **frequencies**, with just one number representing an entire category. One option for gathering such data is *Analyze/Descriptive Statistics/ Frequencies*. Another is *Analyze/Descriptive Statistics/Crosstabs*.

In Variable View create a variable, for example 'tree', again with the Value column assigning the value 1 with the label 'left' and 2 with 'right'. Then create another variable called 'frequency'. In Data View, put the values – here, 1 and 2 – under the 'tree' heading and under the frequency heading. Type the number of times each value was selected. With 13 against 17 from 30 observations we enter:

Image 8.2

	tree	frequency	va
1	1	13	
2	2	17	
3			
4			
5			
6			
7			
8			
9			
10			

Data View | Variable View

Most important: Select *Data/Weight Cases*. Press the 'Weight Cases by' button and transfer 'frequency' to the Frequency Variable box. Then click 'OK'.

Image 8.3

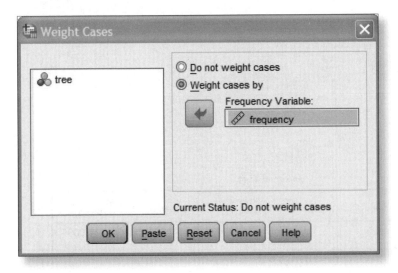

Analysis

Select *Analyze/Nonparametric Tests/Legacy Dialogs/Binomial*. Transfer 'tree' to the Test Variable List. *Leave the small 'test proportion' box at .50 (that is, 50/50).* Click 'OK' to start the test.

Let us take our example of 30 people finding their way past the clump in the tree. For interest's sake, enter 15 for each condition – in other words, a 'fifty-fifty' scenario:

Image 8.4

	tree	frequency	var
1	1	15	
2	2	15	
3			
4			
5			
6			
7			
8			
9			
10			

Data View | Variable View

Image 8.5

Binomial Test

		Category	N	Observed Prop.	Test Prop.	Asymp. Sig. (2-tailed)
tree	Group 1	left	15	.50	.50	1.000[a]
	Group 2	right	15	.50		
	Total		30	1.00		

This should be the result of your analysis. $p = 1$ is what would be predicted as the random scenario (where a 50/50 ratio is expected). The observed proportion is also 50:50, so unsurprisingly, the test is not significant.

Now we try our 17:13 scenario; $p = 0.585$, still insignificant. Again, out of interest, enter the reverse, with 13 above and 17 below: the result is the same, both results being the two sides of the same coin.

Another example: Would you consider buying X product? Out of 100 customers, 67 said yes. 100–67 = 33; 33 people wouldn't buy it. So, with frequencies of 67 and 33, we get a reading of .001 two-tailed.

Dichotomies repeated – the McNemar test

Where we have paired responses, for example people are asked their opinion, yes or no, before a debate and afterwards, we can use the McNemar test. The basic point is that the two conditions, before and after, must use categorical data (and be *correlated*, that is, related to each other). The McNemar is often used in medicine; for example, whether or not children are liable to bad colds, monitored at the age of 12 and then at the age of 14 (Bland, 2000). Another example is to test whether or not a particular symptom exists in a set of individuals, before and after the use of a particular drug.

Raw data
If we want to enter data directly, we want two columns of data, with category numbers, looking like this:

Image 8.6

	before	after
1	1	1
2	1	1
3	1	1
4	1	2
5	2	2
6	2	2

Use *Analyse/Descriptive Statistics/Crosstabs*. Put one variable in 'Rows' and 'one variable in 'Columns', press the statistics box and select 'McNemar'.

Summary data

If we just wish to enter the frequencies, we use Variable View to create two variables for names, adjusting the Type to 'String' (which automatically makes them Nominal) and a 'Frequency' variable, set to zero decimals.

Image 8.7

	Name	Type	Width	Decimals	
1	Before	String	8	0	
2	After	String	8	0	
3	Frequency	Numeric	8	0	
4					

Use *Data/Weight Cases*, select 'Weight cases by' and put 'Frequency' in the Frequency Variable box, then press 'OK'.

This means that, when we enter our data in Data View like this,

Image 8.8

	Before	After	Frequency	
1	Yes	Yes	20	
2	Yes	No	2	
3	No	No	16	
4	No	Yes	12	

the cross-tabulation uses the frequency column. (Alternatives to Yes and No could be Present and Absent for symptoms, or Vulnerable/Resistant and so on.)

Use *Analyse/Descriptive Statistics/Crosstabs*. Put one variable (for example Before) in Rows, the other (for example After) in Columns, press the statistics box and select 'McNemar', 'Continue' and 'OK'. After looking at a case summary to check that we have got the frequencies right, we see a cross-tabulation of the data and then the McNemar significance statistic of .013, $p < .02$ two-tailed. There is a significant difference between the 'Before' and 'After' conditions.

More than two conditions – the Chi Square goodness of fit test

In the case of 40 people being observed turning left or right at the end of a supermarket aisle, we may expect product placement to influence the outcome. Let us say that the difference is 26:14 and we believe that an organised promotion is working well for one side, against a random shelf arrangement on the other. Then the binomial test would tell us whether or not 26:14 is significantly different from chance.

As it might be more realistic to bring in 'straight ahead' as a direction, let us extend our analysis to three conditions.

(A methodological point: yes, I know some people may reverse back up the aisle and I could have four conditions, but the relatively small numbers, with all too clear a difference in the frequency count, would distort the test. It is perfectly valid to exclude these observations as long as the rationale is clear and the decision is recorded for future scrutiny. It would not be valid, however, if I did it just to 'get significance'.) Let us have a bigger sample:

Input process

Table 8.1

Left	Right	Forward	
80	28	42	Total: 150

In Variable View, create two variables, Direction and Frequency. Give the Direction variable three levels, with 'Values' set to 1 = Left, 2 = Right and 3 = Straight. Enter the data in Data View:

Image 8.9

	Direction	Frequency
1	1	80
2	2	28
3	3	42

Select *Data/Weight Cases* and make 'Frequency' the transfer variable; this means that the analysis will use the numbers from the Frequency variable.

Analysis

Then select *Analyze/Nonparametric Tests/Legacy Dialogs/Chi square*, where you transfer the 'Direction' variable to the Test Variable List.

Image 8.10

Direction			
	Observed N	Expected N	Residual
Left	80	50.0	30.0
Right	28	50.0	-22.0
Straight	42	50.0	-8.0
Total	150		

You will become accustomed to the Chi square calculation comparing the observed with the expected numbers, which is its essence. The expected frequencies of 50.00 per category represent the total of 150 divided by the 3 conditions. We can see big differences, especially between 'Left' and its expected value. (There are times when you might want to change the 'Expected Values' in the dialog box from 'All categories equal' to specified values – for example, in studies involving genetics – but, for our current purposes, let us stick with random values.)

The test statistics follow on: Chi square is a very large 28.96, with a *p* value of .000 There are highly significant differences: $p < .0005$ (A note at the bottom of this output reminds us that Chi square calculations generally require frequencies of at least 5 per cell.)

Another example would be a poll of 105 people, asking which social ill is the worst (note that this is exclusive). Crime = 35; Global warming = 37; Immigration = 33. (We could have had a fourth or fifth: insurance companies? advertising?) The expected frequency is 35 per category (105/3) and as suggested by the closeness of all the categories to the expected frequency, any difference is insignificant; $p = 0.892$. The good citizens will be bolting their doors and calling for tougher immigration legislation as the fresh water diminishes and the tides rise....

An important methodological point is that significance in this test merely shows that a non-preference hypothesis must be rejected. It does not demonstrate that one particular choice is strongest. One method of dealing with this would be to create a dichotomy, by putting the strongest option as 'Option A' and the others into 'Option B', and returning to the binomial test. Let us return to our shelf directions – it would be quicker to enter the data via the second, summary data, method, as described in the discussion of the binomial test. Make 1 = 'Left' as one value of a variable (for example 'Directions') and 2 = 'Other' as the second. On the 'Frequency' variable, 'Left' would be given 80 again, with 'Other' becoming 70 (28 + 42). In this case, however, the difference is not significant, so while you may be sure that there are significant factors involved relating to direction, it is not possible to say that this is all one way.

The relationship between variables – the Chi Square test of association

This test examines the relationship between variables. As well as the points about nominal data and exclusivity mentioned previously, it should also be noted that there should be at least 20 observations in the sample, with at least 5 in each category.

Let us extend our supermarket example: we may want to find out if gender interacts with how the goods on offer are presented – or perhaps men and women have a tendency to walk in different directions?

	Males	Females
Left	46	42
Right	11	15
Forward	23	17

Input process

In Variable View, name the variables Gender, Directions and Frequency. The 'Type' for Gender and Directions should be converted to 'String' (for words). Frequency only requires a change to Decimal = 0 for the sake of neatness.

In Data View, enter the data thus, ensuring that the spelling and case are identical throughout.

Image 8.11

	Gender	Directions	Frequency
1	Males	Left	46
2	Males	Right	11
3	Males	Forward	23
4	Females	Left	42
5	Females	Right	15
6	Females	Forward	17

Then select *Data/Weight Cases*. Select '*Weight Cases by*' and then transfer the Frequency variable to the 'Frequency Variable' box. Click 'OK'. (This procedure is not needed if you are dealing with raw data, case by case, as opposed to collated frequencies.)

Analysis

Select *Analyze/Descriptive Statistics/Crosstabs*. In the Crosstabs dialog box, transfer the category with the larger number of levels (here, Directions) to the Row(s) box and the one with the smaller number (Gender) to the Column(s). We do it this way round to avoid unwieldy wide tables. Press the 'Statistics' button and select 'Chi square' and 'Phi and Cramer's V'. After 'Continue', press 'Cells' and select 'Observed', 'Expected' and 'Round cell counts'. Click 'Continue' and then 'OK' in the Crosstabs dialog.

From the output, it is generally worth checking the Case Processing Summary to check that the number of cases is correct.

Directions * Gender Crosstabulation			Gender		Total
			Females	Males	
Directions	Forward	Count	17	23	40
		Expected Count	19.2	20.8	40.0
	Left	Count	42	46	88
		Expected Count	42.3	45.7	88.0
	Right	Count	15	11	26
		Expected Count	12.5	13.5	26.0
Total		Count	74	80	154
		Expected Count	74.0	80.0	154.0

The differences between the observed and expected counts are the point of Chi square. Differences, if they exist, may well show up on the cross-tabulation table. In this case, you will find that the Chi Square Tests output shows a large, non-significant statistic (.481). The null hypothesis is upheld; we have no evidence to support a relationship between gender and the direction taken in supermarkets (although as usual, this is a fictional data set).

Another example of examining the significance or otherwise of the interaction between variables is that of the relationship between having seen a promotion and concern over an issue. Here, we can use a 2 by 2 option, using the same procedures as above.

Table 8.2

		Have you seen the promotion about this issue?	
		Yes	No
Are you concerned with this issue?	Yes	18	12
	No	12	30

Image 8.13

	Awareness	Concern	Frequency
1	Seen	Worried	18
2	Seen	Serene	12
3	Not seen	Worried	12
4	Not seen	Serene	30

Image 8.14

Awareness * Concern Crosstabulation

			Concern		Total
			Serene	Worried	
Awareness	Not seen	Count	30	12	42
		Expected Count	24.5	17.5	42.0
	Seen	Count	12	18	30
		Expected Count	17.5	12.5	30.0
Total		Count	42	30	72
		Expected Count	42.0	30.0	72.0

As the cross-tabulation table shows, there are clear differences between the observed results and the expected results. These differences are significant:

Image 8.15

Chi-Square Tests

	Value	df	Asymp. Sig. (2-sided)	Exact Sig. (2-sided)	Exact Sig. (1-sided)
Pearson Chi-Square	7.112[a]	1	.008		
Continuity Correction [b]	5.878	1	.015		
Likelihood Ratio	7.168	1	.007		
Fisher's Exact Test				.015	.008
N of Valid Cases	72				

a. 0 cells (.0%) have expected count less than 5. The minimum expected count is 12.50.

b. Computed only for a 2x2 table

We are interested in the significance statistic on the top row, .008, $p < .01$ two-tailed. (Fisher's Exact test is for small data sets. Just how small is subjective, but some authorities suggest where any cell has a frequency of 5 or less.)

As the result is a significant one, it is worthwhile considering the effect size, using either Phi or Cramer's V, which we would then encounter in the 'Symmetric Measures' table. In this case, both have a value of .314 with an approximate p value of .008.

Effect size for the Chi Square test of association

For 2 x 2 tables, as in this case, use Phi. With contingency tables larger than 2 x 2 Cramer's V is preferred.

Opinion is divided on how to use these statistics. Some report the value (here, .314) as a correlation coefficient. My advice is to square Phi or Cramer's V, giving an effect size that also shows the proportion of the variance taken up by the effect size.

Take the value, here .314, and square it: .314 x .314 = .098.

The following descriptions of effect size are recommended (Kinnear and Gray, 2004):

< 0.01 (under 1 % of the variance) = Small
0.01 to 0.10 (1 to 10% of the variance) = Medium
> 0.10 (over 10% of the variance) = Large

Our figure of .098 is almost .1 which counts as a medium sized effect.

Although there are clear advantages in being able to look for differences between observed and predicted values (the bigger difference, the better), the more groupings of variables we have, the less meaningful any interpretation becomes. As with other areas of statistical testing, try to select meaningful relationships rather than just dredging for materials to test.

Talking point

There are times when data is 'unquantifiable'. When the data is unreliable, no degree of mathematical sophistication can fail to be undermined. Similarly, if there is no way of establishing a sensible 'starting point' or rationale for analysis, then quantification is pointless.

I would merely point out, however, that there are times when those who declare a topic to be immeasurable may be arguing from a viewpoint of personal preference rather than methodological certainty.

Let me take their side for a while, however. A hermeneutic approach is applied to an interview. That interview may give insights into what may lie behind wads of data. It may also be important to find out if such a viewpoint is shared – returning eventually to quantification in order to demonstrate this – and as a starting point for empirical investigations in new directions.

Without a qualitative focus, how could you decide which of hundreds of thousands of potential experiments are worth conducting? Essentially, there should be a relationship between statistical work and an interpretative focus. Should these be divorced, however?

This test table refers to *frequencies of observations* within *categories* of a sample.

Table 8.3

Number of variables	Number of conditions	Focus	Test
One	2 (dichotomy)	Differences	Binomial test
One	2 (repeated dichotomy)	Correlated differences	McNemar test
One	More than 2	Difference	Chi Square goodness of fit
Multi-variable	2 or more	Interaction between variables	Chi Square test of association

Chapter 9
Correlations, regression and factor analysis

Correlation

Returning to data with measurable differences, we may wish to examine the relationship between one variable and another, its **correlation**. A correlation is summarised by a statistic known as the **correlation coefficient**. This statistic runs from +1 (a perfect positive correlation) through 0 (completely random) to –1 (a perfect negative relationship).

The following numbers and scatter plots will illustrate these.

Table 9.1

1	1
2	2
3	3
4	4
5	5

These two columns of numbers are exactly the same, for example, the same people scoring identically on a measure on two occasions. This can be represented visually using a scatter plot on a spreadsheet such as Microsoft Excel or OpenOffice Calc Chart Wizard or using SPSS Graphs.

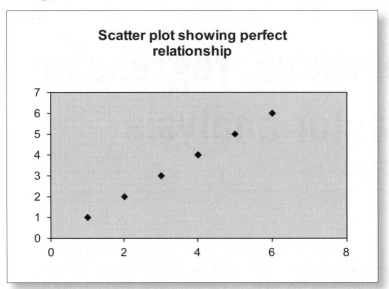

Scatter plot showing perfect relationship

This forms a perfect positive correlation; when statistically analysed it would produce a correlation coefficient of 1. Although you would not expect a perfect relationship in the course of research, a similar slope to this would indicate a positive relationship between two variables.

Table 9.2

1	5
2	4
3	3
4	2
5	1

Now we juxtapose the inverse, a negative relationship; the higher the score on one of the measures, the lower the score on the other one.

Image 9.2

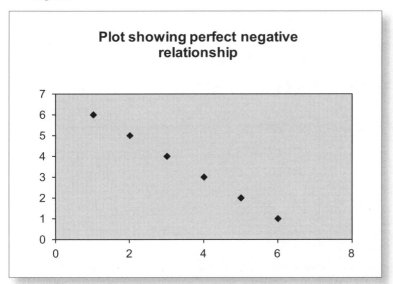

A similar slope, but this time rising from right to left, indicates a negative relationship between two variables. This example is a perfect negative correlation; statistically, this would produce a correlation coefficient of –1.

The numbers on the next chart were randomly generated. No sensible line could go through this set of relationships. With more numbers involved, a globular cluster would be typical.

Image 9.3

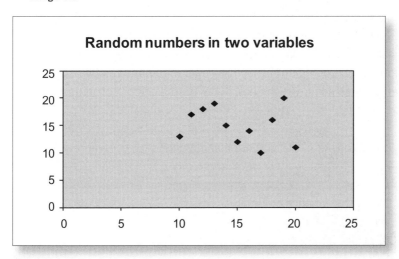

In case you want to reproduce this, the random numbers used were:

Table 9.3

80	83
10	70
84	79
42	98
13	62
76	12
28	29
97	87
12	62
98	44

A random relationship is likely to have a rather small correlation coefficient, possibly close to zero. Conversely, the significance value would be very high.

Effect size and correlations

The correlation coefficient is generally reported as r. If you are not provided with the effect size, then it is simple to work it out for yourself. You multiply r by itself to get **r squared** (or r^2). So if *r* is 0.4, then r squared is 0.4 x 0.4 = 0.16. Note that negative correlations turn positive when squared; so *r* = −0.4 also becomes 0.16. (Some calculators can't multiply negative values; in such a case, just multiply positive values, such as 0.4 x 0.4 to get the correct results.)

Some people mistake the '*p* value' for the measurement of the strength of the relationship; it is, in fact, an assessment of whether or not an effect is 'real' (that is, significant) as opposed to an irrelevant mixture of variables. Similarly, although the correlation coefficient r may be a useful guide to relative effect size, r^2 is the effect size itself, which shows how far the effect accounts for the **variance**.

The following descriptions of effect size are recommended for correlations (Kinnear and Gray, 2004):

< 0.01 (under 1 % of the variance) = Small;
0.01 to 0.10 (1 to 10%) = Medium;
> 0.10 (over 10% of the variance) = Large.

Two conditions tested for a relationship (correlation)
- *Spearman, a non-parametric test, or*
- *Kendall's tau b, a non-parametric test*

As discussed previously (Chapter 4), a non-parametric test does not concern itself overmuch with the nature of the data. This is just as well here, as we are first going to ask it about the perfect positive relationship, the perfect negative one and the pair of variables with random scores.

Input process
In Variable View, create suitable variable names for each of the paired conditions. (We have six, as we are examining three unrelated pairs of numbers.) Set 'Decimals' to zero for neatness; for speed, you can copy the zero value from one cell to the others.

Image 9.4

	Name	Type	Width	Decimals	Label	Values
1	Positive1	Numeric	8	0	Perfect positive A	None
2	Positive2	Numeric	8	0	Perfect positive B	None
3	Negative1	Numeric	8	0	Perfect negativ...	None
4	Negative2	Numeric	8	0	Perfect negativ...	None
5	Random1	Numeric	8	0	Random A	None
6	Random2	Numeric	8	0	Random B	None
7						

Enter the data in Data View.

Image 9.5

	Positive1	Positive2	Negative1	Negative2	Random1	Random2
1	1	1	1	6	80	83
2	2	2	2	5	10	70
3	3	3	3	4	84	79
4	4	4	4	3	42	98
5	5	5	5	2	13	62
6	6	6	6	1	76	12
7	.	.	.	.	28	29
8	.	.	.	.	97	87
9	.	.	.	.	12	62
10	.	.	.	.	98	44

We could have saved time by entering data directly into Data View, with automatically created provisional variable names. However, such a habit can lead to terrible errors in any but the simplest of exercises.

Analysis

Select *Analyze/Correlate/Bivariate*. We don't want the Pearson test, the default option, as this is a parametric test (to be used shortly), so deselect this and select the Spearman option. (Kendall's tau–b is also usable in a non-parametric context; it gives somewhat different results to Spearman and some statisticians favour it, for example, Arndt et al, 1999. Use it as well if you like.) Transfer the first two variables of interest to the box on the right and click 'OK'.

(I know we could have put all of the conditions into the box at one go but, for the moment, I think we should forgo possible complications in the output.)

In this case, the read-out gives the expected 1 for a perfect positive for both statistics, with –1 being given when we try out the perfect negative correlation. No significance value is given for either extreme.

This is a continuum of correlation coefficients:

Table 9.4

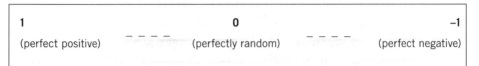

1	0	−1
(perfect positive)	(perfectly random)	(perfect negative)

Let us look at the read-out for our randomised variables:

Kendall's *tau b* statistic gives the correlation coefficient .045 – very near zero – while Spearman's statistic, *rho*, is at .158, still very small. The significance values (.857 and .663) are very high, a long way indeed from the $p < .05$ or lower that we usually seek.

Now, let us approach real life. In a survey, people may express confidence in the government, running from very high at rating 5 to very low at rating 1. They may also be rated in terms of confidence in the future, from not confident at 1 to very confident at rating 5.

The scale 'Confidence in the Government' (suggesting that this is at low ebb) is:
1, 5, 4, 2, 2, 3, 1, 1, 3, 2

The scale 'Confidence in the Future' (here, people seem unsure) is:
5, 4, 5, 3, 1, 2, 4, 3, 2, 2

Image 9.6

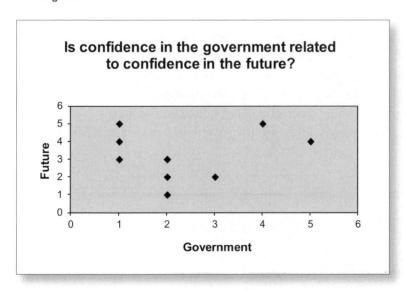

Having seen a fairly bitty scatter plot chart – I have used a spreadsheet's graphics as this is more straightforward than that of a statistics package – we subject the figures to our non-parametric tests. The Spearman test coefficient turns out to be about –.06, obviously small. The significance level is 0.875, very big; any effect is clearly a matter of chance. (The tau b readings, close to –.08 and .776, are quite similar.)

Now compare the 'Confidence in the Future' ratings with the following salaries for each person (in thousands): 28, 30, 25, 27, 18, 20, 15, 24, 18, 22.

Image 9.7

m1	Random2	Govt	Future	Salaries
80	83	1	5	28
10	70	5	4	30
84	79	4	5	25
42	98	2	3	27
13	62	2	1	18
76	12	3	2	20
28	29	1	4	15
97	87	1	3	24
12	62	3	2	18
98	44	2	2	22

Let us assume that the researcher had predicted beforehand that salary would be positively associated with confidence in the future. After selecting *Analyze/ Correlate/Bivariate*, transfer the future and salaries variables into the box on the right and select 'one-tailed'. Given the small numbers, $p < .05$ was an acceptable level (5 in 100 chance of a fluke finding) and we may argue that theoretical likelihood means a (less rigorous) one-tailed level of analysis would be acceptable.

Image 9.8

Correlations

			Confidence in future	Salaries
Kendall's tau_b	Confidence in future	Correlation Coefficient	1.000	.483*
		Sig. (1-tailed)	.	.032
		N	10	10
	Salaries	Correlation Coefficient	.483*	1.000
		Sig. (1-tailed)	.032	.
		N	10	10
Spearman's rho	Confidence in future	Correlation Coefficient	1.000	.572*
		Sig. (1-tailed)	.	.042
		N	10	10
	Salaries	Correlation Coefficient	.572*	1.000
		Sig. (1-tailed)	.042	.
		N	10	10

*. Correlation is significant at the 0.05 level (1-tailed).

As can be seen, we can reject the null hypothesis at $p < .05$ one-tailed. The two-tailed variation, with the significance values doubling, would not have been seen as significant (although this would probably be because of our limited numbers). Significant correlations have been marked with an asterisk; in the event of $p < .01$, a double asterisk would be used by SPSS.

Did you check the scatter graph for this example? A mild slope can be discerned.

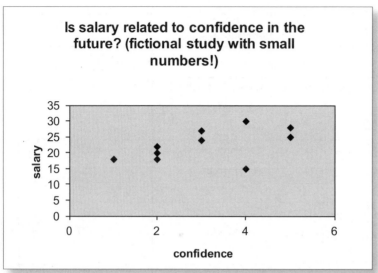

Is salary related to confidence in the future? (fictional study with small numbers!)

A cautionary note: Why do I insist upon looking at scatter plots in addition to using a test? The reason is that the correlational tests here (non-parametric and parametric) are *linear*. They assume a relationship that runs in one direction, whether positive or negative. If you run a test without looking at a scatter plot as well, there is the danger of assuming significance or lack of it from test results which are completely misleading. Below are two examples of non-linear correlations.

The first is a real-life error by the author. I examined a friend's blood pressure readings against time (thanks, you know who, for allowing me to reproduce this evidence of my impulsive nature). The coefficient was −0.16, with a two-tailed critical value of .3 – this non-significant result came as a surprise to both of us as we had expected some sort of pattern to emerge. Then, I remembered....

Image 9.10

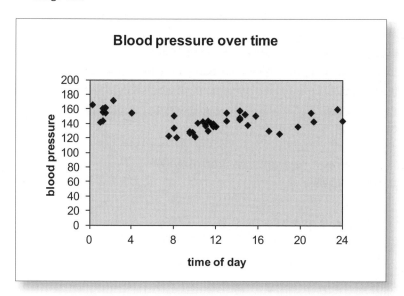

The graph's wave-like formation suggests a tendency towards higher blood pressure readings in the early afternoon and also at night. So there is an effect, but it is not a linear one. While the graph is informative, I should not have used a linear test with this information; the correlations were, of course, meaningless.

Another non-linear example may be familiar to students of stress and to sports fans.

Image 9.11

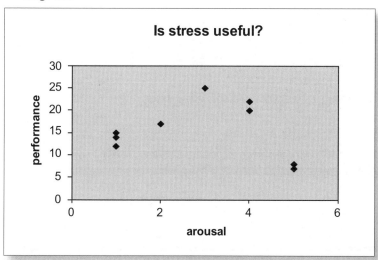

This (fictional) grading of performance against high and low graded stress levels is indicative of what is known as the Yerkes–Dodson Law (Yerkes and Dodson, 1908). Although high stress may damage performance, some degree of stimulation seems necessary. Again, this non-linear effect would emerge from a graph, but if the data were subjected to a correlational test, parametric or non-parametric, any results would be erroneous. Essentially, 'curvilinear' relationships should not be subjected to these tests and we should, of course, examine our data graphically before considering testing.

Two conditions tested for a relationship (correlated)
• Pearson, a parametric test

Input process
Open a new file and create two variables in Variable View, say 'PaperA' and 'PaperB'.

Then enter the following data sets in Data View as parallel columns:

If you reopen the examination retakes file, you should find the following numbers in the third column: 62, 56, 40, 37, 62, 56, 68, 55, 68, 60. You can copy these numbers into 'PaperA' or type them in afresh.

If you remember, this last examination retake represented a significant improvement in examination scores. Perhaps this result was seen as a lucky accident: we would want to test **reliability** (whether or not a measure is consistent over time). We want to use the same students but if we used the same test, as 'test-retest', this could be inappropriate because of practice effects, so we use a parallel test, which asks different questions about the same taught material. Type in the new scores under 'PaperB': 65, 55, 39, 43, 66, 54, 73, 58, 72, 64.

Save this file as 'Parallels', as we will need this again later.

Analysis
If we use a scatter plot to examine the relationship between these two variables, we see a clear positive slope.

Image 9.12

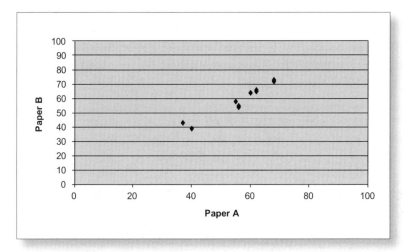

Before using a parametric test (here, the Pearson), we need to check for normal distribution. Use *Analyze/Descriptive Statistics/Explore*, transferring both variables (papers A and B) into the 'Dependent List' box (they are both 'Scale' measures), and then pressing the 'Plots' button to select 'Normality plots with tests'.

The Shapiro–Wilk test is non-significant, so we do not have to worry about non-normal data (use Kolmogorov–Smirnov with 50 or more cases). If the data had proven unsuitable, we would have used Spearman or Kendall's tau b.

The statistics read-out tells us that the two sets of figures have similar means (56.4 and 58.9) and each has a similar range (the difference between the minimum and the maximum figures). This suggests but does not prove a relationship between the two sets of data.

If you want to create a more manageable version of the statistics, select *Analyze/ Descriptive Statistics/Descriptives*.

Then select *Analyze/Correlate/Bivariate*. As we are using normal data, we want the Pearson test option. Let us say that previously we had not been at all sure of whether or not the results would be close: use the two-tailed option. Transfer both variables to the variables window. Go into 'Options' and select 'Means and standard deviations' (you are likely to want to report these) followed by 'Continue', then 'OK'.

The correlation coefficient is .971, which is highly significant: $p < .0005$ – there is very little chance of this result being a fluke. Clearly, the examination results are very reliable. (If you calculate the square of the correlation, .971 x .971, you get the effect size, a statistic called r^2 ('R Squared'): at .943 this represents almost 95% of the variance; in other words, only just over 5% of the variance from the mean is likely to be due to chance factors.)

For an example of a non-significant result using Pearson's correlation, try comparing the first two variables in the examination retake file (reproduced here):

52, 53, 47, 40, 48, 45, 52, 47, 51, 38 : 60, 34, 38, 52, 54, 55, 36, 48, 44, 56

Let us return to our earlier example. The correlation coefficient of .971 meant a large effect size, .943. What if we had a more modest effect, for example, with a coefficient (r) of .55, giving an effect size (r x r) of 0.3025, just 30% of the variance? Various ideas emerge from this. If the rest of the variance is random 'noise', could the research model be improved, made more reliable? Is there another factor at play which could contribute to our understanding of the effect? Is the significant result meaningful in real-world terms, and should we invest in it? These questions become less academic when we look at multiple regression.

As a building block, however, we first need to consider regression as a concept.

Regression

Simple linear regression (two conditions)
When we looked at the scatter plot charts for significant relationships between two sets of data, a slope could be ascertained, representing the relationship. A line can be drawn through the incline (assuming it makes sense when considering the real-world context) and even extended, taking us into the realms of prediction.

Image 9.13

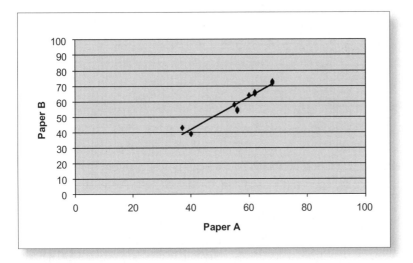

The chart above shows the two closely correlated variables from our 'Parallels' file, with a trend line attached.

By looking for where the X variable meets the intercept (the line), we can see what value is expected from the Y variable. However, as real life does not always allow for such simplicities, regression is more often used for creating models of what is likely to work in theory than to make real-life predictions.

It should be noted that regression in SPSS is for parametric data. (You will find a test for more rough-hewn data in another statistics package, the inexpensive StatsDirect. The appropriate test is found there by selecting *Analysis/Regression & Correlation/Non-parametric Linear Regression.*) However, as in the case beneath, survey ratings can usually be dealt with using SPSS, especially if the data is within reasonably normal bounds.

Let us consider a simple fictional situation of some individuals with debt-related problems. Levels of debt (the predictor) are likely to affect the take-up of assistance from debt relief services (the criterion).

Input process
The data is entered in the same way as correlations. In Variable View, enter 'Debt' and 'Help'. To make these more understandable, Labels could be 'Debt Level' and 'Help Take-up Likelihood'.

In Data View, enter the following for 'Debt': 1, 1, 1, 2, 2, 2, 3, 3, 3, 4, 4, 4, 5, 5, 5 (high ratings indicate worse problems) and under 'Help', the rated likelihood of their looking for help (5 meaning they have declared themselves certain to seek help): 3, 1, 1, 2, 1, 2, 3, 2, 3, 2, 3, 4, 4, 5, 5.

Analysis

Check for normal distribution using the Shapiro–Wilk test (Kolmogorov–Smirnov for 50 or cases), using *Analyze/Descriptive Statistics/Explore*, using the 'Plots' button to select 'Normality plots with tests'. Put both variables into the 'Dependent List'. In this case, there is no reason to assume non-normality and we can proceed. (From the *Explore* statistics, you may want to report the means and standard deviation statistics.)

We are interested in how far the level of debt is likely to affect the take-up of help. So debt is our predictor (in SPSS, 'independent variable') and likely take-up of help is our outcome (or criterion or dependent variable). In everyday terms, will debt levels be a useful guide to the likely take-up of counselling services?

Select *Analyze/Regression/Linear*. Move 'Debt level', the predictor, to the Independent box and 'Likely help take-up', the criterion, to the Dependent box.

Image 9.14

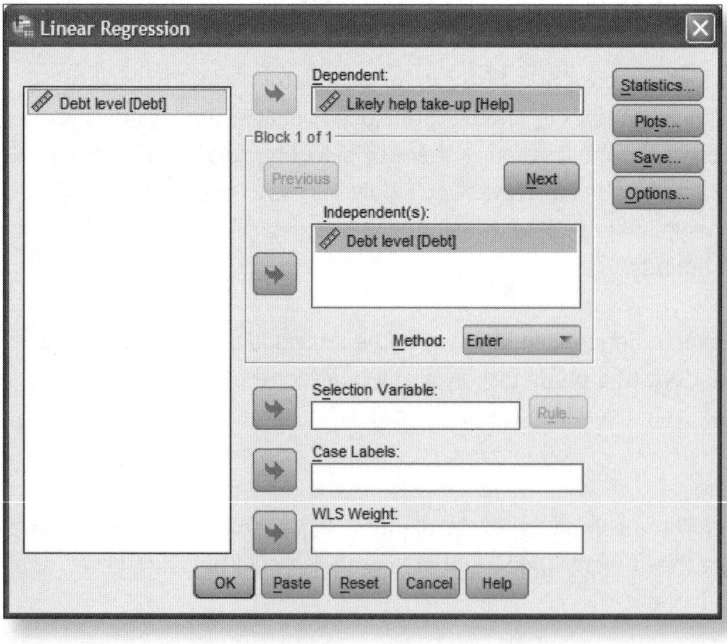

Press 'OK'. The output *p* value will be .000 which has the highly significant critical value of $p < .0005$ The standardised coefficient is a very large .804.

When it comes to regression, we do not need to square the coefficient to get the effect size, as SPSS shows us this in the 'Model Summary'. *R Square* is .647, but we generally accept the slightly more modest *Adjusted R Square* (.620), which in this case is very large.

Effect size for regression
A small effect size is smaller than .01 (1% of the variance); a medium size is 0.01 to 0.10 (1 to 10%) and large is greater than 0.10 (more than 10% of the variance).

Now create a scatter plot (you should find that spreadsheet charts are easy to create and adjust). The scatter plot is the only way to be sure of a truly linear relationship between the two variables.

Image 9.15

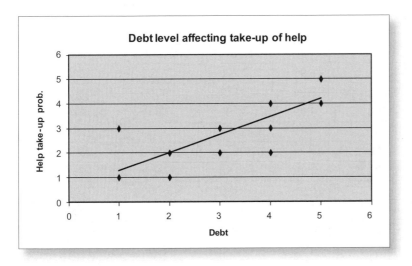

Looking at the intercept, from 'Chart/Add Trendline' on another package (for example, Microsoft Excel), it seems possible (if we had more data, we would be more confident) that people with greater problems are more likely to seek help, while this may be somewhat less likely at an intermediate level; perhaps information about services needs to reach the intermediate problem group before they get into further trouble....

Let us go into more detail with another example of regression, using the commercial data set below. For the moment, let us just look at Sales and Price. Is there a meaningful relationship between these variables, and can we make predictions about how well a product will sell if we change the price? (Before anybody blames me for their financial demise, these are fictional figures. 'Pile High, Sell Cheap' works in some markets and not in others....)

In Variable View, enter Shop, Sales, Price, Instore, Street and Radio, perhaps with Labels of 'Shop Number', 'Sales Numbers', 'Item Price', 'Street Promotion' and 'Local Radio'. While making Decimal zero on most variables, leave 'Price' with 2 decimal places. Then enter the numbers in Data View as below and save the file, perhaps as 'Sales'; the additional data will be used for multiple regression shortly.

Table 9.5

Shop	Sales	Price	Instore advertising	Street promotion	Local radio
1	8600	24.99	2180	6400	12000
2	9100	18.99	2200	7800	11500
3	9400	24.99	2220	6800	12400
4	9500	24.99	2160	7000	13500
5	9800	18.99	2220	6500	13200
6	10700	18.99	2170	5000	13500
7	11200	18.99	2280	6800	13200
8	11400	18.99	2500	7200	13500
9	11400	18.99	2200	6000	13500
10	11700	18.99	2250	7400	12900
11	3800	30.99	2190	5000	11000
12	4900	30.99	2250	7500	12000
13	6100	24.99	1180	5400	11900
14	6500	30.99	2250	6000	12500
15	6900	30.99	2170	8200	12100
16	7300	30.99	2180	6500	14000
17	7400	20.99	2255	6100	12200
18	7600	30.99	2250	6800	12300
19	7800	18.99	2200	6000	13300
20	8100	20.99	2240	6900	10000
21	11800	30.99			

It should be noted that the data above is not all of a normal distribution as the author wished to achieve various effects with a small data set.

Let us go straight to some statistical analysis. Select *Analyze/Regression/Linear*. Move 'Sales' to the Dependent box and 'Prices' to the Independent box, ensure the method box reads 'Enter'. Press 'OK'.

The Correlation Coefficient reads −0.605; the negative is fine, representing an inverse relationship: lower prices, higher sales. $p < .01$. The effect size, *Adjusted R Square*, is .333, meaning that the relationship between these two variables only accounts for a third of the variance. We shall look at the implications of this shortly.

Now, let's look at a chart.

Image 9.16

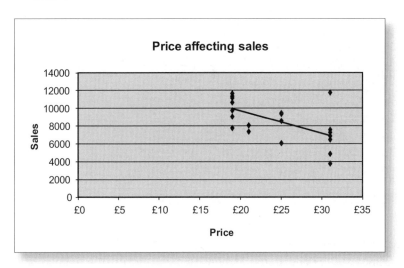

Apart from anything else, we want to make sure that the relationship is linear. It is linear; the left to right downward slant indicates a negative correlation. Another problem emerges, however: an outlier. This is, of course, why you are generally advised to look at the graphical data first. One coordinate is well away from the other data and is theoretically dubious: one shop is selling at the highest price and yet is also selling well. Perhaps it is a shop for the extremely well-heeled. Let's not go there.

During data exploration, removing real information (as opposed to data entries) just because it is inconvenient to you is unforgivable. We are now, however, in the business of making predictions, so it is reasonable to remove the outlier to improve the prediction model. We are interested in the generality of usual behaviour.

Now to use linear regression analysis without the outlier. *Remove shop number 21 from Data View* (including the column number on the far left, to stop the statistics package from referring to 'missing data').

If we look at the chart with just the 20 cases, it looks more tightly knit.

Image 9.17

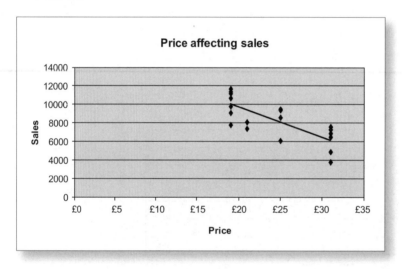

Now for analysis without the outlier: select *Analyze/Regression/Linear*. Move 'Sales' to the Dependent box and 'Prices' to the Independent box, ensure the method box reads 'Enter', then press 'OK'.

The correlation is now –.767 which gives an effect size (*Adjusted R Square* in 'Model Summary') of .566. With much more of the variance accounted for, over half, we have a more valid tool for prediction. It may now be possible to interpolate from X to Y, in other words to be able to generalise that, by adjusting the price, it is likely to have a predictable effect on sales.

Multiple regression – multiple predictor variables against one criterion variable

Returning to our shop data, we may ask if price by itself is the only significant factor in determining the number of sales. Multiple regression allows us to build a *model* for effective prediction. We are interested in two main issues:

- Does the addition of extra variables make an appreciable difference to predictions?
- And if so, are some variables more useful than others?

Input process

As with correlations and simple regression.

Analysis

Select *Analyze/Regression/Linear.* Put Sales as the 'Dependent Variable' (Y axis) – remember the outlying 21st case should have been removed – then select Price, Instore Advertising, Street Promotion and Local Radio as 'Independent Variables'. Ensure the method box reads 'Enter' and click 'OK'.

Image 9.18

Model		Unstandardized Coefficients		Standardized Coefficients	t	Sig.
		B	Std. Error	Beta		
1	(Constant)	-821.105	4592.545		-.179	.860
	Item Price	-289.770	51.597	-.677	-5.616	.000
	Instore advertising	.892	1.171	.098	.762	.458
	Street promotion	.558	.329	.215	1.697	.110
	Local radio	.849	.275	.377	3.082	.008

Coefficients[a]

a. Dependent Variable: Sales numbers

The coefficients are quite informative: Price, in an inverse way ($r = -0.677$), is seen to be significant (that is, not a chance effect), but so is Local Radio.

To find out the answer to our first question, whether or not additional variables make an appreciable difference to our predictive model, see the 'Model Summary': $R = .892$ and the effect size of .741 (*Adjusted R Square*) accounts for 74% of the variance. As the effect size of the simple regression was .566, this model is clearly a more effective one. In other words, we would do well to consider other factors in addition to price when predicting sales.

Before trying anything else, it may be worth checking for statistical safety. Run the regression again but this time press the 'Plots' button in order to examine the residuals:

Image 9.19

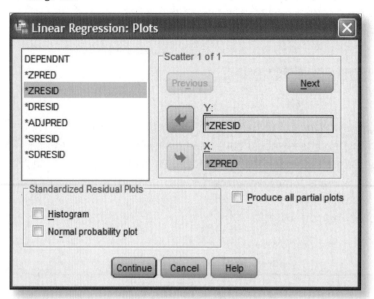

Image 9.20

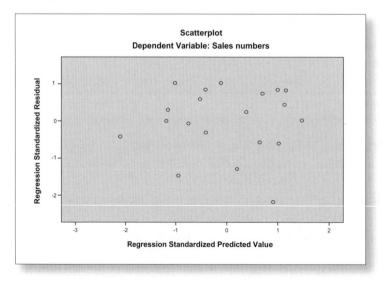

The residuals, essentially errors, are randomly spread, which is what we want.

Also calculate '*Collinearity*': essentially, high collinearity means that variables are over-correlated against each other, possibly meaning that they may be measuring the same underlying construct; in such a case, we probably need to get rid of unnecessary variables. (Rather than fishing for results, you should only include variables that 'make sense'.) Run the regression calculation again, this time pressing the 'Statistics' button and selecting 'Collinearity diagnostics'. Consult the Coefficients output box, where you will find 'Collinearity Statistics' columns on the far right. It is desirable to have a high Tolerance factor, approaching 1; as the Tolerance column shows figures between .821 and .939, this is good. We also want a low VIF – variance inflation factor – where not being far above 1 is good; the VIF figures are also satisfactory, being between 1.065 and 1.218.

Returning to the significance levels, it looks like a worthwhile move to refine our model by removing Instore Advertising and Street Promotion as less influential factors. So now we go back and perform multiple regression with just Price and Local Radio as predictors: our two factors account for considerably more of the variance than the simple model.

This time, $R = .851$, with an effect size (*Adjusted R Square*) of .691, almost 70% of the variance. We do not seem to have lost much by removing the other predictor variables while gaining considerable clarity by having only two. Having said that, you could always look for another relevant factor.

The procedure we have followed above is called Standard Multiple Regression, also known as Simultaneous Multiple Regression, as all variables are examined at the same time. This is usually the only method you will need. Another method is known as Sequential or Hierarchical, which is used when you believe that the order of variable entry is important; this is the reason for the 'Method' box in the Linear Regression dialog box. As with standard regression, only more so, a theory of what is being examined is necessary to guide the technique's usage. (One source of further information is Miles and Shevlin, 2000.)

Partial correlation – 'partialling out'
In various reports, you will come across the phrase 'controlled for'. This is useful for situations where variables are likely to overlap each other. This sort of analysis can be used to inform our use of regression analyses and also which variables to exclude

in factor analyses (to be dealt with later in this chapter). Here, let us control for age – statistically removing its influence – when looking at examination reliability.

Input process

As with correlations and regression.

Use the 'Parallels' file, relating to two similar examination papers, that we used with the Pearson test. Let us add a new variable in *Variable View*, 'Age', adding the following figures in Data View: 16, 21, 17, 16, 20, 18, 30, 22, 27, 23.

Analysis

Select *Analyze/Correlate/Partial*. Move Test Paper A and Test Paper B to the Variables box and Age to the 'Controlling for' box. If we are expecting a positive result (as opposed to a negative correlation) and previous research, or experience of the student group in question, indicates that older students will generally put in a better performance and that this is the direction in which the results are tending, then we should go for a one-tailed significance reading. Otherwise, we should opt for the more rigorous two-tailed test. Given the small data set, it seems reasonable to set our expectations of the acceptable level of significance to $p < 0.5$

We can look at the means at the same time as the rest of the test by using the Options button; as well as 'Means and standard deviations', select 'Zero-order correlations' in order to compare the controlled for results with the original (zero-order) correlations. 'Continue' and 'OK'.

The outputs will show a Correlations box. The 'zero order' correlations in the first half of the table show us the coefficients without the partialling out. Each variable on the left is shown in turn correlated with the variables listed at the top. The results of 1.000 are, of course, where a variable is correlated with itself.

Here, the Pearson test ($r = .971$, $p < .0005$ one-tailed), indicates an immensely strong relationship between the performances on the two papers. However, it is also clear that there is a relationship between each of the tests and the age of the students. Even if we had used a two-tailed test and the significance readings had doubled to .024 for paper A and .016 for paper B, both would have remained significant for our purposes.

In the lower section comes our partial coefficient ($r = .942$). The strong relationship between our parallel papers still exists, so we can be confident in their reliability (unless something untoward is happening at the test venue). However, it is somewhat smaller and it reduces the effect size: if we square the earlier and later coefficients for the test papers, we get $r^2 = .942$ and .887 In this case, we have a more accurate assessment, but the difference is not great; this is not always the case.

As suggested earlier, partialling out can help us to work out which factors to exclude in factor analysis. Before we get to factor analysis, however, we need to consider multiple correlation.

The multiple correlation matrix
You may study the pattern of relationships between more than two variables.

Input process
As in correlations and regression.

Analysis
One simple way of examining multiple correlations is to put more than two variables in *Analyze/Correlate/Bivariate*. If you do this using the data from our multiple regression exercise, you will find that the output is not very readable. However, this method has the advantage of offering non-parametric tests (Spearman and Kendall's tau b) as well as parametric.

A rather neater version can be found using *Analyze/Dimension Reduction/Factor*. Press the 'Descriptives' button and select 'coefficients' for the correlation matrix; you may also choose 'significance levels' as in the output below. (You can safely ignore the other output unless or until you read about factor analysis.) Do note, however, that the test used here will be parametric (Pearson) and so is not suitable for more rough-hewn data sets.

Image 9.21

Correlation Matrix						
		Sales numbers	Item Price	Instore advertising	Street promotion	Local radio
Correlation	Sales numbers	1.000	-.767	.320	.200	.534
	Item Price	-.767	1.000	-.116	.036	-.229
	Instore advertising	.320	-.116	1.000	.363	.172
	Street promotion	.200	.036	.363	1.000	-.071
	Local radio	.534	-.229	.172	-.071	1.000
Sig. (1-tailed)	Sales numbers		.000	.085	.199	.008
	Item Price	.000		.313	.440	.166
	Instore advertising	.085	.313		.058	.234
	Street promotion	.199	.440	.058		.383
	Local radio	.008	.166	.234	.383	

Two common features of correlation matrices may be seen. First, where a variable is matched against itself, a perfect correlation (1.000) is observed. Second, the two triangular halves of the correlation matrix on either side of the perfect correlations are mirror images of each other, so you only need to pay attention to one of these triangles of data (the lower half is probably easier to look at). The data triangles make it easier to look for meaningful patterns of relationships.

Please also note that the lower table offers a one-tailed significance reading. Unlike the straightforward bivariate correlation, it is expected that with multiple correlations you will already have some idea of what you are analysing. We will now develop this argument.

There is a danger in examining ever greater numbers of variables. The more correlations you calculate, the greater the probability that some apparently significant relationships are, in fact, chance results. If we decide on a significance level of $p < .05$ then each test has a one-in-twenty chance of being a fluke. Calculation of multiple correlations makes it quite likely that you will unwittingly report fluke results as if they were meaningful. (This same warning applies to other tests; running a large series of t tests in order to 'see what is significant' is a well-known error.) So 'dredging' for data, just finding out what will emerge from throwing a lot of variables together, is ill advised.

One way of tackling this problem is a strictly statistical approach. We can raise the bar for which correlations we are willing to accept.

One highly conservative method of doing this is the Bonferroni technique: you simply multiply a correlation's p value by the number of comparisons to get an adjusted p value. If we take our multiple regression example using all the variables there, we find that there are ten pairings, ten sets of results.

The radio promotion p value is $p = 0.008$, $p < .01$; our comparisons numbering 10, the Bonferroni would give 0.08, non-significant. This is rather harsh and – this is the real world entering our calculations – almost certainly wrong. The Bonferroni is particularly fierce when applied to a large number of tests. My own method, mentioned earlier, the number of pairings minus .5, still provides an insignificant result: $0.008 * 9.5 = 0.076$. Either we need to invent a new, more sensitive test, or do the sensible thing and reduce the number of variables to those which we are truly interested in.

Image 9.22

Correlation Matrix

		Sales numbers	Item Price	Local radio
Sig. (1-tailed)	Sales numbers		.000	.008
	Item Price	.000		.166
	Local radio	.008	.166	

If, however, we reduce our examination to sales, price and radio promotion, as recommended towards the end of the multiple regression example, we are only using 3 comparisons, giving an adjusted p value of $3 \times .008 = 0.024$, $p < .05$.

As I have suggested earlier, we could use a slightly milder way of allowing for multiple correlations, by multiplying by the number of conditions minus .5. In the case of 10 pairings, we would multiply by 9.5, giving a still non-significant .076 but using the reduced pairings, we would be multiplying by 2.5 giving $p = 02$, $p < .05$. (If you used this approach to adjusting significance values, you would need to report it.)

Overall, I suggest that significance adjustment is not a suitable fix without having made some judgements about reducing the number of variables under examination.

The situation becomes even muddier when you consider clearly significant correlations with relatively small effect sizes. A coefficient of .44. for example, has an effect size accounting for less than 20% of the variance. Is that significant in the everyday sense of the word? This conflict between statistical significance and meaningfulness is a common problem and will vary according to context.

Real-world analyses may be less clear than in our example. As well as concerns over useful degrees of magnitude, the use of several correlations, with a range of decent sized coefficients, may render 'eyeballing' of the correlation matrix a hopeless enterprise. Although you will still find that statistical output will rarely allow you to dispense with subjective judgement, some help with decision making can be made with the assistance of Exploratory Factor Analysis.

Factor analysis – a data reduction methodology

Exploratory factor analysis

Factor analysis extracts underlying variables, or **dimensions**, from data. The reader may find this section more difficult than the earlier ones; believe it or not, you will find far more complex explanations of factor analysis elsewhere....

The basic point of exploratory factor analysis is to take several correlations and reduce a bulky conglomeration of variables into hopefully meaningful components, or factors. Factor analytic techniques try to find a structure in the relationships between variables, reducing the number of variables into a smaller number of components. If, for example, survey respondents declare a liking for several variables, you may want to find out if there are a few common attitudes which account for many of the responses.

As usual, there are real-world considerations. Avoid the poor practice of lumping together all the variables from a large study. Put in those variables which you think are likely to be relevant. Also, note that the results should be inter-correlated to some extent: if there is no relationship, then there will be no common factors. On the other hand, too high a correlation between two variables may indicate that they measure the same thing; one of these variables should be removed before a factor analysis is conducted. There is serious debate about whether or not factors are merely statistical artefacts rather than meaningful entities (for example, Temple, 1978). In practical terms, this can be resolved to some extent; as is usual when using statistical techniques, a lot depends upon having a sensible rationale for action rather than just pressing the button to see what happens.

To make life even more interesting, the term 'factor analysis' is used both as a generic term for the extraction of underlying variables from data, as discussed above, and also as a specific group of techniques. However, the following very brief explanation of the three major steps involved gives you the basics.

First, a correlation matrix is formed from the data (as we looked at in the previous section). Second, factors are extracted. Third, the factors can be rotated, in order to try to find a clearer way of viewing the factors. A brief discussion of **rotation** can be found in the statistical theory box later in this chapter.

The data below consists of 15 rows, representing observations (individuals, shops or other objects) and the 12 variables, A to L. The latter could be measures of business data, individuals' performance on different tests and so on. We want to see if there are any common underlying variables, how many there are, and how far each contributes to the variance.

Table 9.6

A	B	C	D	E	F	G	H	I	J	K	L
82	92	61	28	25	16	79	54	60	43	28	61
41	44	67	51	81	45	62	61	32	57	54	67
41	72	71	74	79	30	85	57	40	51	41	39
93	84	58	43	42	15	70	70	76	69	14	20
86	92	48	54	36	26	72	69	67	59	14	26
39	53	51	75	48	42	94	84	69	58	19	39
54	45	89	54	56	42	89	60	49	47	35	40
88	98	58	27	35	11	70	62	72	57	15	33
78	97	69	53	41	12	72	67	54	46	26	42
66	92	63	76	60	28	56	43	21	39	80	83
72	95	55	79	39	35	60	53	32	53	60	74
71	87	65	73	70	13	80	65	64	65	20	33
76	80	52	67	60	16	67	52	53	54	51	56
47	61	76	45	79	36	56	63	56	55	38	51
84	81	56	73	61	48	47	39	14	34	75	87

Input process

The initial data entry is made as with correlations and regression. In Variable View, enter 'Case' and the 12 variables (A, B, C and so on). Set all 'Decimals' to 0. In Data View, enter numbers 1 to 15, and the data for the variables as above.

There are three points to be made about the raw data. There should be at least 100 observations (we have 180), although it has been suggested that a cautious interpretation may be made with over 50. There should also be 5 times as many subjects (rows) as variables, although, with less than 100 observations, this should be extended to between 8 and 10 rows for each column (this rule is ignored here for brevity's sake). Also, it is helpful to place variables that you think are related side by side.

Analysis

Select *Analyze/Dimension Reduction/Factor.* In the factor analysis dialog box, transfer the relevant variables to the Variables box on the right.

The following images are suggested settings for this (adapted from Kinnear and Gray, 2004) and will be discussed as we look at the read-out:

Image 9.23

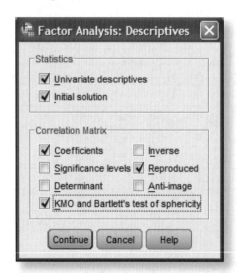

Image 9.24

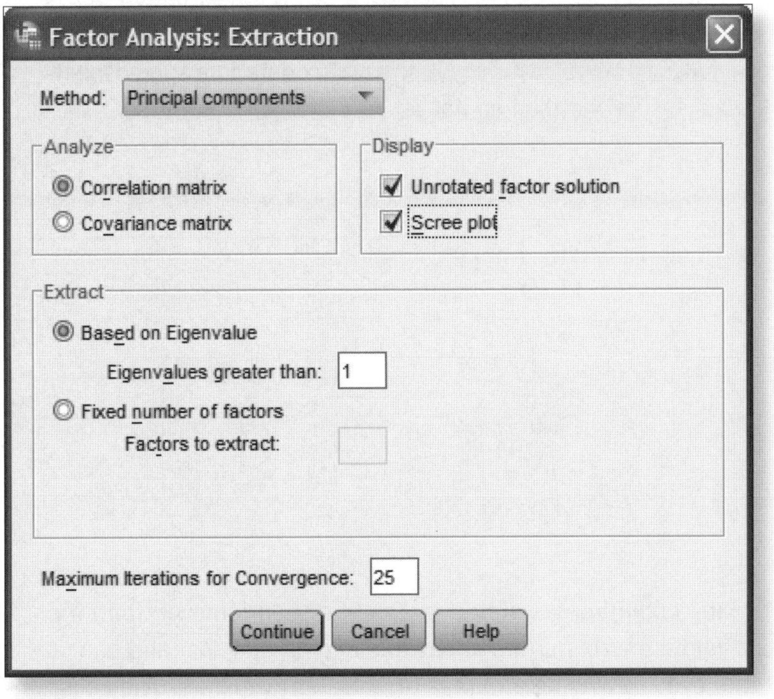

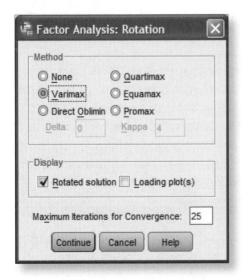

Image 9.25

The initial descriptive statistics output provides a basic summary of each variable, with the mean, standard deviation and number of cases. The next output box is the correlation matrix, as discussed in the multiple correlations exercise. I suggest an additional technique, however, transferring the matrix data to a spreadsheet ('paste special', using text rather than an image).

Image 9.26

	A	B	C	D	E	F	G	H	I	J	K	L
A	1											
B	0.80	1										
C	-0.46	-0.49	1									
D	-0.34	-0.09	-0.15	1								
E	-0.68	-0.59	0.45	0.40	1							
F	-0.61	-0.70	0.20	0.40	0.44	1						
G	-0.30	-0.28	0.19	-0.05	-0.17	-0.17	1					
H	-0.22	-0.27	-0.07	-0.21	-0.17	-0.15	0.64	1				
I	0.23	0.10	-0.15	-0.53	-0.42	-0.58	0.58	0.79	1			
J	-0.01	-0.10	-0.18	-0.17	0.02	-0.33	0.33	0.72	0.72	1		
K	-0.18	-0.06	0.05	0.52	0.40	0.51	-0.65	-0.83	-0.95	-0.68	1	
L	-0.10	0.01	-0.05	0.36	0.20	0.47	-0.65	-0.79	-0.88	-0.74	0.92	1

The upper half of the computer-generated matrix has been removed from the chart above, as a whole matrix mirrors about the leading diagonal and can play tricks with the eyes, providing a mirage of imaginary clusters. The cells have also been conditionally formatted; any figure above .3 or below −.3 is in a darker font. Positive correlations of less than .3 and negative correlations larger than −.3 tend not to be meaningful in this context. (Another rule of the principal components default extraction setting is that some correlations should be larger than .3.)

Previously, I recommended the practice of placing variables which are particularly likely to be related to each other into adjacent columns of the raw data. This allows easy viewing of any correlation clusters. Guessing which variables are closely related before subjecting the data to analysis is always a good idea. As previously discussed, you should have some rationale behind your data selections. But, in the case of the correlation matrix, failure to align the variables will require an even more intense eyeballing of the data. When looking at data with which you are familiar, the nature of the factors should become clearer.

In this case, we can see that variables K and L are highly correlated, with strong negative relationships with several other variables; often a construct may be partially defined by opposites. A and B are also highly correlated, with a grouping of positive relationships.

Also appearing in the output is the KMO (Kaiser–Meyer–Olkin Measure of Sampling Adequacy) and Bartlett's test of sphericity (as previously mentioned, sphericity is a statistical assumption for repeated measures). KMO = .320, Bartlett is significant at a *p* value of .000 ($p < .0005$). For our input data to be suitable for a satisfactory factor analysis, the KMO statistic should be greater than .5. Given my small number of rows, this shortcoming is not surprising; perhaps I shouldn't have had so many variables (columns). The test of sphericity significance level should be smaller than .05, which it is.

The next output, 'Communalities', refers to how much of the variance has been accounted for by a variable. The readings here will range from .598 in the case of variable G through to .968 for variable K.

Image 9.27

Total Variance Explained

Component	Initial Eigenvalues		
	Total	% of Variance	Cumulative %
1	5.280	43.996	43.996
2	3.228	26.897	70.893
3	1.200	10.004	80.897
4	.837	6.972	87.868
5	.725	6.039	93.907
6	.259	2.160	96.067
7	.184	1.532	97.600
8	.138	1.148	98.747
9	.076	.633	99.380
10	.040	.336	99.716
11	.032	.269	99.985
12	.002	.015	100.000

Extraction Method: Principal Component Analysis.

Components 1 to 12 on the left of the 'Total Variance Explained' box are generated by the software and are not of importance, except in showing the order of size of potential components, from largest to smallest. Any components could conceivably be considered to be factors and we need a way of deciding on a cut-off. As will be discussed, this can be a matter of judgement, dependent on known attributes, but the reading of Eigenvalues, shown in the 'Total' columns, is a useful statistically based cut-off procedure. Generally speaking, we only take account of components with Eigenvalues of 1 or more. This is called Kaiser's criterion (Kaiser, 1960). According to this criterion, there would appear to be three discernible factors.

Factors 1, 2 and 3 are seen to account initially for 44%, 27% and 10% of the variance, accounting together for almost 81%. Rotation of the factors (the 'Rotation Sums of Squared Loadings' output) adjusts the variance estimates to 40%, 30% and 11%.

Image 9.28

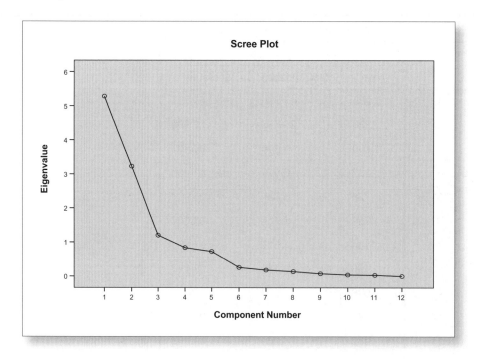

The Scree plot (Cattell, 1966) is another popular guide to deciding how many factors are meaningful. The last point before the slope starts to level off is considered usable. The guidance from the Eigenvalues seems to be borne out.

The next item on the output is the Component Matrix, which appears as three columns. The matrix columns refer to the three components estimated by the program. What are called 'loadings' are correlations between the factors and the test. Some sort of pattern emerges, with some variables scoring more highly in different columns, each of which represents one underlying dimension. Generally, we are interested in statistics greater than .3 and, in negative relationships, smaller than –.3. The figures from the component matrix are best transferred to a spreadsheet and formatted to highlight the groupings. Some analysts prefer .5 or even .6 rather than a .3 cut-off; there does not appear to be any rule determining the size of the cut-off (Pohlmann, 2004).

Image 9.29

	1	2	3
A	-0.29	**-0.89**	-0.06
B	-0.18	**-0.90**	0.09
C	0.16	**0.55**	**-0.72**
D	**0.51**	0.19	**0.69**
E	**0.48**	**0.63**	0.05
F	**0.63**	**0.54**	0.14
G	**-0.60**	**0.48**	0.00
H	**-0.79**	**0.46**	0.23
I	**-0.98**	0.05	-0.02
J	**-0.72**	0.27	**0.35**
K	**0.97**	-0.13	0.07
L	**0.91**	-0.24	0.01

The next output box provides a set of 'Reproduced Correlations' in its upper half which are related to the loadings. The lower box, 'Residual', carries a warning: there are 25 residuals with significance values of greater than 0.05. We actually want residuals to be as small as possible to show a good 'fit' between the original matrix and the reproduced one. So this is another sign that perhaps some variables should not be there.

Image 9.30

	A	B	C	D	E	F	G	H	I	J	K	L
A		-0.05	0.03	0.02	0.03	**0.06**	-0.05	-0.03	-0.01	0.05	-0.01	-0.06
B	-0.05		**0.10**	**0.12**	**0.07**	-0.12	0.05	-0.02	-0.03	-0.02	-0.01	-0.04
C	0.03	**0.10**		**0.15**	**0.06**	-0.10	0.02	-0.02	-0.03	0.04	0.01	-0.06
D	0.02	**0.12**	**0.15**		0.00	-0.12	**0.17**	-0.04	-0.03	-0.08	0.00	-0.07
E	0.03	**0.07**	**0.06**	0.00		-0.21	-0.19	-0.09	0.02	**0.18**	0.01	-0.09
F	**0.06**	-0.12	-0.10	-0.12	-0.21		-0.04	**0.08**	0.00	-0.06	-0.05	0.03
G	-0.05	0.05	0.02	**0.17**	-0.19	-0.04		-0.05	-0.04	-0.23	0.00	0.02
H	-0.03	-0.02	-0.02	-0.04	-0.09	**0.08**	-0.05		0.00	-0.05	-0.02	0.05
I	-0.01	-0.03	-0.03	-0.03	0.02	0.00	-0.04	0.00		0.01	0.01	0.02
J	0.05	-0.02	0.04	-0.08	**0.18**	-0.06	-0.23	-0.05	0.01		0.04	-0.02
K	-0.01	-0.01	0.01	0.00	0.01	-0.05	0.00	-0.02	0.01	0.04		0.01
L	-0.06	-0.04	-0.06	-0.07	-0.09	0.03	0.02	0.05	0.02	-0.02	0.01	

A formatted spreadsheet version of the residuals, with > .05 converted to bold font, suggests that variables B and C are particularly suspect. A look at the original correlation matrix, especially the formatted version, suggested that these variables did not correlate particularly well with the rest of the data set.

Image 9.31

Rotated Component Matrix[a]

	Component		
	1	2	3
A	-.096	-.932	-.011
B	-.170	-.897	.154
C	-.070	.541	-.740
D	-.263	.403	.734
E	-.180	.775	.055
F	-.336	.748	.175
G	.732	.199	-.149
H	.934	.113	.051
I	.898	-.343	-.173
J	.823	-.031	.200
K	-.916	.274	.232
L	-.916	.142	.176

Extraction Method: Principal Component Analysis.
Rotation Method: Varimax with Kaiser Normalization.

a. Rotation converged in 4 iterations.

The 'Rotated Component Matrix' output gives us the clearest information. Below, we see a more clear-cut version where I have used a spreadsheet to format the numbers which are larger than .5 and smaller than −.5 as a cut-off. This is rather more effective than > .3 and < −.3.

Image 9.32

	1	2	3
A	-0.10	**-0.93**	-0.01
B	-0.17	**-0.90**	0.15
C	-0.07	**0.54**	**-0.74**
D	-0.26	0.40	**0.73**
E	-0.18	**0.78**	0.06
F	-0.34	**0.75**	0.18
G	**0.73**	0.20	-0.15
H	**0.93**	0.11	0.05
I	**0.90**	-0.34	-0.17
J	**0.82**	-0.03	0.20
K	**-0.92**	0.27	0.23
L	**-0.92**	0.14	0.18

The three factors appear in sharper relief (although there are still questions, at least relating to B and C, as members of group 2).

Finally, the Component Transformation Matrix appears on the output screen, which relates to how the components have changed since rotation, but I do not think it worthy of consideration (which is, of course, a researcher's way of saying he hasn't a clue about how to read it).

Generally speaking, the evidence suggests that a third factor is likely to have explanatory power. When dealing with variables in real life, however, we are likely to have more of a clue as to what a factor consists of and how important it is. Real-world considerations would be likely to inform us whether or not the smaller factor has any meaning or is merely a mathematical construct.

An example in real life is from a survey of contributors to a charity. Responses to several statements along the lines of 'Leaving me to decide if I wish to give', 'Giving me a choice over the communications I receive' and 'Giving me a choice over how often I am contacted' were grouped together. Another set of strong correlated response ratings linked such statements as 'Thanking me properly for any gift I choose to give', Responding quickly when I contact with a question' and 'Informing me how my money is spent'.

After consideration, it seemed reasonable and understandable to the charity to view two sets of conceptual constructs as relevant. One seemed to be about personal choice. The second factor seemed to be more about customer service. The charity was advised that these factors were likely to be of importance to contributors.

As you might suspect, in spite of all the calculations, exploratory factor analysis has a considerable element of subjectivity, an art as well as a science if you like.

Confirmatory factor analysis

As a relatively advanced technique, CFA is not going to be covered in any detail here (consider using Brown, 2006). Essentially, while Exploratory Factor Analysis (EFA), as above, looks at data in a 'bottom-up' way and attempts to create a model of underlying factors, Confirmatory Factor Analysis works 'top–down'. It uses data to confirm or test models with factors. You can test models against each other, for example. You can test the reliability of a model; in the example given, you might try out new sets of data to see if a two– or three–factor model is the more useful, or if the entire model is misleading (there are certainly grounds for re-running our original EFA with a couple of variables removed).

We used the principal components setting for EFA. In CFA, a factor analysis technique, such as principal axis factoring, is more likely to be selected from the 'Extraction' settings, with rotation methods selected according to situation and theoretical leaning. Often, CFA is part of a broader research methodology known as Structural Equation Modelling (see Kline, 2010).

Statistical theory – look away now!!

Factor analysis – a short technical appendix

Factors – also known as latent variables, dimensions, or core constructs.

Eigenvalue – represents the total amount of variance contributed to by a factor. The use of Eigenvalues of 1 and above is known as the Kaiser Criterion (Kaiser, 1960).

Eigenvalues, however, are a *guide*, particularly for when the divide between potential factors is less than clear. Depending upon the meaningfulness of the potential categories, you could conceivably have argued for four factors in our example. In real-world decision making, the number of factors should be influenced by theory and/or empirical evidence. All other things being equal, however, a theory with fewer factors should be preferred in borderline cases.

Rotation – Whereas the positions of clusters on X and Y axes make a lot of sense in univariate (single variable) statistics, the immediate position of variables in multivariate statistics is not particularly meaningful. The point is that the initial position of a set of factors on graphical 'X Y' axes may not lead to sensible clusters: a three dimensional concept, as it were, is placed on a two-dimensional chart, rendering the direction of the axes largely irrelevant. The constellations of stars could be a useful metaphor: these appear to be real formations but are, in fact, individual stars at diverse distances merely clustered according to the viewer's perspective. Rotation is a legitimate way of adjusting the position of the clusters to achieve '*simple structure*', a tight and meaningful separation of factors (Thurstone, 1947). Simple structure, however, is an elusive concept; before running a factor analysis, you are also presented with the rather complex question of which type of rotation to choose, orthogonal or oblique and so on!

Talking point

We have already established that apparently strong correlations can be coincidental. Do too many tests and that five-in-a-hundred fluke is increasingly likely to occur.

Another perceived weakness of correlations is that they do not prove cause and effect. This is, of course, a problem. As an example, let us say that we have established a reliable relationship between confidence in the government and high levels of spending. Are we sure that perceived stability leads to higher spending? Or could it be that high disposable incomes lead to political complacency?

Or is there a mediating factor which needs to be taken into account, such as unemployment?

One way of sorting out the problem is to run experiments or quasi-experiments. It is not always practical to do so, however. Triangulation of methods can be also be used; different aspects of a problem may be subjected to different forms of analysis to see if the original theory may be disproven. Confirmatory Factor Analysis (see for example, Brown, 2006) could be used to test the given relationship, looking at different variables to examine the direction of an effect or to provide more explanatory models. Methods such as Structural Equation Modelling (for example, Kline, 2010) are also used to examine the direction of correlational effects.

This table of tests of relationships is not exhaustive, but refers to tests used in this chapter.

N.B. Non-parametric tests can be used with 'parametric' data.

Do also note that non-parametric linear regression may be found on some statistical packages, for example, StatsDirect.

Table 9.7

Purpose	Number of variables	Data	Test
Correlation	2	Non-parametric	Spearman/tau b
	2	Parametric	Pearson
	More than 2	Both possible	Multiple correlation
	2, + 1 or more controls	Parametric	Partial correlation
Prediction	2	Parametric	Linear regression
	More than 2	Parametric	Multiple regression
Data reduction	Multi-variable	Parametric	Factor analysis

Chapter 10
Factorial analysis of variance

We now look at analyses of variance which examine two or more factors at once. An interesting feature of this form of analysis is that not only does it look at differences between the levels (conditions) of factors – 'main effects' – but it also looks at 'interaction': possible relationships between factors. Where this book has generally dwelt on differences and similarities separately, we now find both together. The General Linear Model (GLM) underlying factorial ANOVA in fact underlies ANOVA, the t test, regression and factor analysis, allowing such a connection between differences and similarities.

Factorial ANOVA is commonly used for two-way and three-way analyses. *Do note that it is not advisable to extend ANOVA beyond three factors as interpretation is liable to become very difficult.*

Moving the other way, one-way ANOVA can be applied to only two conditions, but the t test tells us what we want to know in this case.

Effect size for factorial analyses of variance

Clark–Carter (1997) recommends 0.01 as a small effect, 0.06 as medium and 0.14 as large. Kinnear and Gray (2004) extrapolate this to: $< .01$, less than 1% of the variance, as small; 0.01 to 0.10 (1 – 10%) as medium; > 0.10 (more than 10% of variance) as large.

Within-subjects two-way ANOVA

This test requires the SPSS Advanced Module. It is recommended that you try out the worked example on within-subjects one-way ANOVA before doing this.

Over the period of a day an experimental visual stimulus was introduced into a home for adults with autism. The research assessed its effectiveness in reducing individuals' stereotypical behaviours (as usual, this is a fictional study). The dependent variable is a scale, with 1 as the lowest possible score and 10 as the highest, indicating the maximum level of the person's usual range of behaviours. One factor is the viewing phase (before the stimulus was introduced, the viewing day, and after the removal of the visual stimulus). The other factor is the time of day the scale was completed (morning or afternoon).

Input process

It is very important to be clear about the structuring of the data. Here, we first separate our data according to the viewing phase factor, and then subdivide it by the other factor, the time factor. Each piece of data then becomes a combination of each level of the different factors:

Table 10.1

	Pre-view (1)		View (2)		Post-view (3)	
Case	a.m. (1)	p.m. (2)	a.m. (1)	p.m. (2)	a.m. (1)	p.m. (2)
1	6	8	4	5	6	8
2	4	5	3	4	4	4
3	9	8	6	5	8	6
4	7	4	7	6	8	8
5	6	7	6	6	7	6
6	7	8	5	7	6	7
7	5	5	4	3	4	5
8	6	8	4	5	5	7
9	4	3	3	4	5	6
10	6	9	4	6	5	8

Notice in particular the order of the columns: 1,1 – 1,2 – 2,1 – 2,2 – 3,1 – 3,2 as this will be very important later on when you transfer variables in the Repeated Measures dialog box.

The subdivisions are then entered vertically in Variable View (the 'Measures' field keeps the default of 'Scale'):

Image 10.1

	Name	Type	Width	Decimals	Label
1	Case	Numeric	8	0	Case number
2	preAM	Numeric	8	0	Pre-view AM
3	prePM	Numeric	8	0	Pre-view PM
4	viewAM	Numeric	8	0	Viewing AM
5	viewPM	Numeric	8	0	Viewing PM
6	postAM	Numeric	8	0	Post-view AM
7	postPM	Numeric	8	0	Post-view PM

The data is then typed into Data View in the order given in the previous table:

Image 10.2

	Case	preAM	prePM	viewAM	viewPM	postAM	postPM
1	1	6	8	4	5	6	8
2	2	4	5	3	4	4	4
3	3	9	8	6	5	8	6

Select *Analyze/General Linear Model/Repeated Measures*. This leads to a dialog box for defining the factors. As usual with SPSS repeated measures be very careful when doing this.

As illustrated in the exercise for Within-Subjects One-Way ANOVA, define the first factor by replacing 'factor 1' with a more meaningful name. Do note that all names in this dialog box must be eight or fewer characters and start with a lower case letter. Then enter the number of levels, and follow this by 'Add'. This time, we repeat this procedure for the second factor, so we should get the image on the left. Then put the dependent variable name into the 'Measure Name' box and press 'Add' to get the right-hand situation.

Image 10.3   Image 10.4

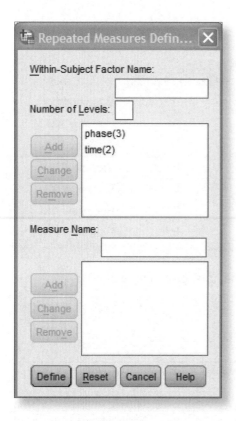
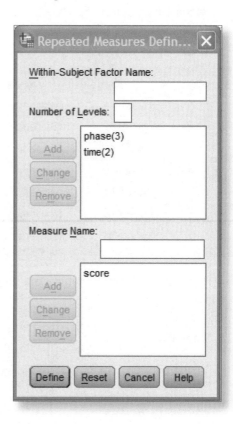

Then press 'Define', which takes us to the Repeated Measures dialog box.

Image 10.5

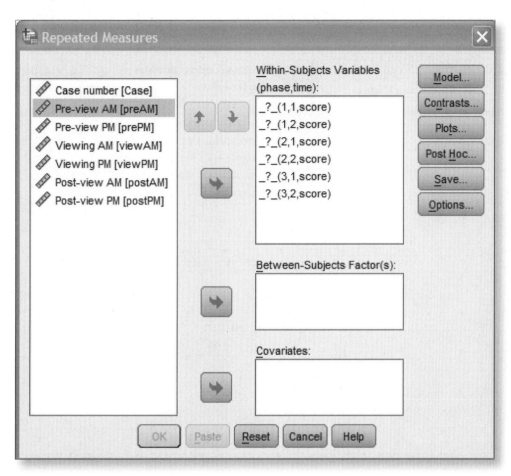

At the top right, you should see your newly defined factors (phase, time). Now you need to take great care. The transfer of the variables to the right must match the numbering system we identified (for example postPM at the bottom should match '3,2'). It is recommended that you practise transferring variables one by one; block transfers can go wrong, especially where there are a larger number of variables. The newly completed dialog box is shown. The up and down buttons allow alterations in order.

Image 10.6

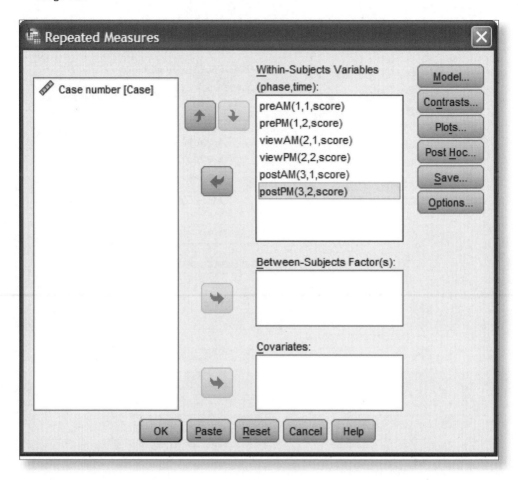

The Between-subjects box is not needed here, but will come into play when we consider mixed design ANOVA. The Covariates box is for factors which are not relevant to the study but which may influence it; please read my reservations about ANCOVA at the end of this chapter before considering using it.

Then press the 'Plots' button, putting the factor with the greater number of conditions (levels) on the horizontal axis, and the other onto 'separate lines'.

Image 10.7

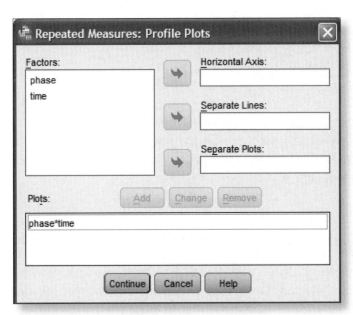

Then click 'Add'. If correct, the 'Plots' box will become populated, like so:

Image 10.8

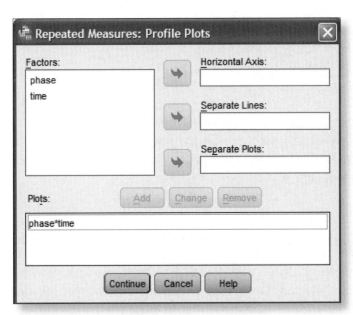

Then press 'Continue' and press the 'Options' button. Put 'phase' into the 'Display Means for' box, select the 'Compare main effects' tick box and select 'Sidak' as the 'Confidence interval adjustment'. Select also 'Descriptive statistics' and 'Estimates of effect size'.

I haven't opted for homogeneity tests because I assume, as recommended previously, that you have already checked that the data is suitable for parametric testing. Press 'Continue'.

Ignore the 'Post Hoc' button, as these tests are not for repeated measures.

Analysis

Image 10.9

Measure: score		
phase	time	Dependent Variable
1	1	preAM
	2	prePM
2	1	viewAM
	2	viewPM
3	1	postAM
	2	postPM

The first output gives you a chance to check that you have defined the factors correctly. The second output gives the mean and standard deviation (*SD*), both of which are normally reported in academic papers. This gives rather lower means for 'Viewing AM' and 'Viewing PM'.

Ignore any output relating to multivariate tests and multivariate contrasts.

The sphericity test is not significant, so the sphericity assumption for repeated measures has not been violated. (There is no test for 'time' as this has only two levels.) In cases when you do get a significant result here, please read the exercise on mixed ANOVA later in the chapter to see what to do.

'Tests of Within-subjects Effects' are our main interest. Read the 'sphericity assumed' line. One of the main effects, phase, appears to be significant, $F = 9.438$, Sig. = .002 – this has a critical value of $p < .01$ – and a very large effect size, Partial Eta Squared = .512 which accounts for more than 50% of the variance. The other main effect and the interaction are not significant.

Ignore the output for 'Tests of Within-subjects Contrasts' and also references to between-subjects effects (non-existent here).

The output called 'Estimated Marginal Means' indicates that the stimulus phase (4.850) appears to be different from the pre- and post-stimulus phases, both of which seem to have rather similar means (6.25 and 6.15 respectively).

The 'Pairwise Comparisons' output will show significant differences between the stimulus phase and both of the other phases ($p = .022$; $p = .001$). There is no significant difference, however, between the pre- and post-stimulus phases. If you had used the Bonferroni correction instead of the Sidak, you would have found the same significance levels. This is often the case, but see the mixed design ANOVA exercise later in the chapter for an instance when this is not so and for a more detailed discussion.

Image 10.10

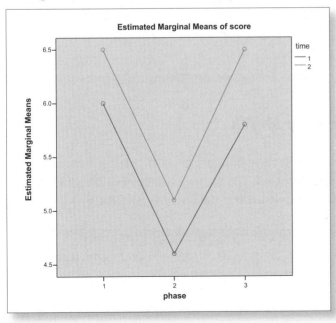

Time number 1 (morning). is the lower of the two 'v' formations. The fact that both 'time' lines head in the same direction means that the 'phase' effect is a 'global' effect. As the lines do not intersect nor do they even tend towards it, there is no sign of interaction.

In general terms, it is worth examining every factorial ANOVA plot with great care.

In this exercise it would appear that the visual stimulus did influence people's behaviour, but the effect did not last after the stimulus was removed.

Within-subjects three-way ANOVA

We could split our data further. If we had an additional factor such as the use or otherwise of a music track at the same time, instead of having 'preAM', 'viewAM', we would have factors such as preAMmusic, preAMnomusic, viewAMmusic and so on. Similarly, the input for SPSS would need to be extended and applied with great care.

Table 10.2

Pre-view (1)				View (2)				Post-view (3)			
a.m. (1)		p.m. (2)		a.m. (1)		p.m. (2)		a.m. (1)		p.m. (2)	
M (1)	NM (2)	M (1)	NM (2)	M (1)	NM (2)	M (1)	NM (2)	M (1)	NM (2)	M (1)	NM (2)

The rhythm would thus be 1,1,1 – 1,1,2 – 1,2,1 – and so on.

Between-subjects two-way ANOVA

Here, we are interested in the effects of different pilots of political broadcasts on individuals' views of a particular policy. The control condition is a broadcast of general interest but without any relevance to the policy in question.

The criterion (dependent variable) comprises the ratings from a short questionnaire, with a rating total of up to 10; higher ratings indicate a positive attitude to the policy. The respondents are different individuals in all conditions.

Table 10.3

Factors		Political broadcast types		
	Political bias	*Broadcast A*	*Broadcast B*	*Control*
A space is left here for a reason (see later exercise)	Pro-government	4,5,6,3,7	3,4,6,1,6	2,3,5,1,4
		5,6,7,4,6	5,7,6,2,4	6,6,4,1,4
	Opposition preference	6,8,7,8,6	3,7,7,6,2	4,6,7,5,1
		8,9,7,6,8	6,8,4,2,6	6,8,3,3,5

Input process

In Variable View, enter 'Case', 'Broadcast', 'Politics' and 'Ratings'. The last label, our dependent variable, would be extended to, say, Survey Ratings for clarity. Decimals should be adjusted to zero. Under 'Values' for Broadcast and Politics, add levels (conditions) for the grouping variables, so Broadcast could have 1 = Broadcast A, 2 = Broadcast B, 3 = Irrelevant; Politics would have: 1 = Pro-government, 2 = Opposition.

In Data View, check the View menu: Value Labels should be set to 'on' (ticked).

This means that if, for example, you type '1' under Politics, it will be converted automatically to 'pro-government', providing the ease and clarity which is really important when handling factorial combinations.

I suggest that you input the data from the table into columns, so the order is as follows:

Table 10.4

Case	Broadcast	Politics	Rating
1–10	(1) Broadcast A	(1) Pro-government	N
11–20	(1) Broadcast A	(2) Opposition	N
21–30	(2) Broadcast B	(1) Pro-government	N
31–40	(2) Broadcast B	(2) Opposition	N
41–50	(3) Irrelevant	(1) Pro-government	N
51–60	(3) Irrelevant	(2) Opposition	N

Here is a snapshot of the data if you have followed this particular format:

Image 10.11

	Case	Broadcast	Politics	Ratings
28	28	Broadcast B	Pro-govern...	6
29	29	Broadcast B	Pro-govern...	2
30	30	Broadcast B	Pro-govern...	4
31	31	Broadcast B	Opposition	3
32	32	Broadcast B	Opposition	7
33	33	Broadcast B	Opposition	7
34	34	Broadcast B	Opposition	6

Data View   Variable View

Analysis

Select *Graphs/Legacy Dialogs/Boxplot*. Click on the 'Clustered' item and then 'Define'. The dependent variable (survey ratings) goes in the 'Variable' box (variable as in 'can be changed', I guess), with the main grouping variable (broadcast type), under 'Category Axis'. The secondary variable (political leanings) goes into the 'Define Clusters by' box. Click 'OK'.

Image 10.12

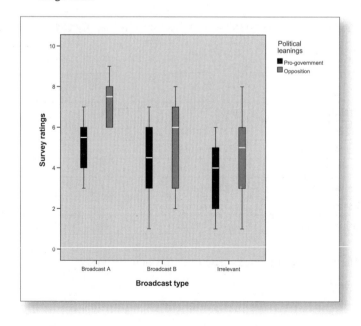

There are no outliers. We get the distinct impression that respondents with oppositional views (the right hand of each pairing) have favourable views of the policy under broadcast A, although the precise logic is uncertain. (Maybe broadcast A works better if people are alienated, or they are looking for a change, or they currently have financial problems, and so on.) It looks possible, however, that people with oppositional views generally respond more positively in all of the conditions – perhaps the auditorium gives them a feeling of unaccustomed wellbeing – but this needs to be checked for significance. It could be that the policy-related pilot broadcasts do not differ significantly from control except in cases where people have an oppositional disposition; again, we need to check.

Select *Analyze/General Linear Model/Univariate*. In the Univariate dialog box, enter Survey Ratings into the Dependent Variable field; place both Broadcast and Politics into the Fixed Factor(s) box.

Don't bother with the other boxes. The Random Factors option is rarely chosen, applying as it does to the use of a random sample of conditions (levels). The Covariate box is for variables which may create 'noise'. However, see the discussion of ANCOVA at the end of the chapter before considering using this.

Open 'Plots'. Put 'Broadcast' in the 'Horizontal Axis' box and 'Politics' into 'Separate Lines'. Then press 'Add' to transfer these into the 'Plots' box. Then press 'Continue' to return to the Univariate dialog box.

Open 'Post Hoc' if you have a variable with three or more conditions (levels). In this case, place 'Broadcast' in the right-hand window and select 'Tukey'. This allows an examination of differences between pairs of conditions within this variable. Press 'Continue' again.

Open 'Options' and select 'Descriptive Statistics', 'Estimates of effect size' and 'Homogeneity tests'. Click 'Continue'. Finally, click 'OK'.

Initially, check the initial summary to check that the correct cases have been analysed (here, the three broadcast types have 20 cases each and the political attitudes have 30 each).

Then check the descriptive statistics. In this case, you will see that the means differ between each broadcast status and between political status within each treatment condition.

The Levene test is not significant, so homogeneity is not a problem.

The next table requires some detailed explanation.

Image 10.13

Tests of Between-Subjects Effects

Dependent Variable:Survey ratings

Source	Type III Sum of Squares	df	Mean Square	F	Sig.
Corrected Model	77.083[a]	5	15.417	4.798	.001
Intercept	1550.417	1	1550.417	482.550	.000
Broadcast	47.433	2	23.717	7.382	.001
Politics	25.350	1	25.350	7.890	.007
Broadcast * Politics	4.300	2	2.150	.669	.516
Error	173.500	54	3.213		
Total	1801.000	60			
Corrected Total	250.583	59			

a. R Squared = .308 (Adjusted R Squared = .244)

We can ignore the first two rows. We are interested in 'Broadcast' and 'Politics', the main effects, and the interaction, 'Broadcast * Politics'. The *F* values are generally reported in academic results. The differences between the broadcast treatment conditions are significant, $p < .002$; politics also differs dependent upon condition, $p < .01$. The interaction, however, with its small F value, is not significant. (*Adjusted R Squared* is a measure of how good the overall model is; the nearer to 1, the better.)

So while we know that broadcasts make a difference and so does the political status, we can not say that there is a reaction between the two effects. We can examine the differences between the specific broadcasts with the Tukey test in the 'Multiple Comparisons' output table. Broadcast A is more effective than either Broadcast B or the control condition ($p < .05$ and $p < .002$). Broadcast B is inferior to Broadcast A (one significance asterisk in the table is adjacent to a negative difference in the means) but is not significantly better than the control.

This impression is reinforced by the means being placed into subsets from the Tukey test. Where means share a subset, their means are not significantly different.

Image 10.14

Survey ratings

Tukey HSD[a,b]

Broadcast type		Subset	
	N	1	2
Irrelevant	20	4.20	
Broadcast B	20	4.75	
Broadcast A	20		6.30
Sig.		.599	1.000

It would appear to be that people with oppositional sympathies are more likely to be influenced by such broadcasts – or perhaps are likely to respond better when in difficult circumstances – but that the choice of broadcast is not a politics–dependent one, that is, not 'horses for courses'. Broadcast A clearly conveys the policy more effectively. Broadcast A does appear to have a greater effect, however, when applied to individuals who are against the government. (Please note: as usual, this is a wholly fictitious data set.)

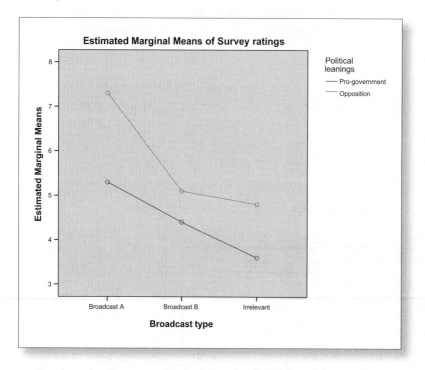

The broadcasts are on the horizontal axis, with political leanings on the vertical, the upper line representing those with oppositional tendencies, who tended to respond with higher ratings for the broadcasts in general.

The failure of the lines to cross each other demonstrates the lack of an interaction; we are unable to say with confidence that a particular broadcast needs to be deployed according to which type of political leanings the viewers have.

More interesting, however, is the position of broadcast A on the lower scoring Pro-government line. It is still higher with those favouring the status quo than the other broadcast conditions even when watched by people with oppositional views. Broadcast A would appear to be particularly effective if the respondents are already well-disposed to the government.

Between-subjects three-way ANOVA

Table 10.5

Factors		Political broadcast types		
Gender	**Political bias**	**Broadcast A**	**Broadcast B**	**Control**
Male	Pro-government	4,5,6,3,7	3,4,6,1,6	2,3,5,1,4
Female		5,6,7,4,6	5,7,6,2,4	6,6,4,1,4
Male	Opposition preference	6,8,7,8,6	3,7,7,6,2	4,6,7,5,1
Female		8,9,7,6,8	6,8,4,2,6	6,8,3,3,5

Input process

We have now added gender to our broadcast and politics factors. This becomes a new variable Gender in Variable View. On this occasion, to fit in with the table, I suggest providing Values with 1 = male and 2 = female. If you followed the previous input system, then moving down the cases in Data View, you would alternate 5 males and 5 females, going down each broadcasts column, and then on to the next broadcasts column. Again, for ease of input, I would suggest that *View/Values* are set to 'on' so that you can type the number and get the whole name appearing.

Image 10.16

	Case	Broadcast	Politics	Ratings	Gender
1	1	Broadcast A	Pro-govern...	4	male
2	2	Broadcast A	Pro-govern...	5	male
3	3	Broadcast A	Pro-govern...	6	male
4	4	Broadcast A	Pro-govern...	3	male
5	5	Broadcast A	Pro-govern...	7	male
6	6	Broadcast A	Pro-govern...	5	female
7	7	Broadcast A	Pro-govern...	6	female
8	8	Broadcast A	Pro-govern...	7	female
9	9	Broadcast A	Pro-govern...	4	female
10	10	Broadcast A	Pro-govern...	6	female
11	11	Broadcast A	Opposition	6	male
12	12	Broadcast A	Opposition	8	male

This is a screenshot of the first 12 cases.

Analysis

Use the same procedure as for the preceding two-way example, but add 'Gender' to the 'Fixed Factors' box.

To save trees, I will only cite output which is additional to or somewhat different from the previous exercise.

Check the Between-subjects Factors table to ensure that you have the correct number of males and females (30 each). The descriptive statistics tell us that females have higher scores than males; this would appear to be the case throughout the table, but we will need check if this is significant.

The differences across the broadcast conditions are significant, $p < .005$; political status also differs dependent on condition, $p < .01$, with effect sizes of about 22% and 13%. Gender difference proved not to be significant. (I even checked gender by itself, using a Mann–Whitney test of the scores: not significant. A correlational test will show, in fact, that there is something of a relationship between the two conditions, so the variances were similar in their relationship to the ratings, in spite of the differences in score size.)

None of the interactions, including a new, three-way interaction (Broadcast, Politics and Gender), were significant.

Gender did not turn out to be a significant issue in this study.

Mixed design two-way ANOVA

Mixed designs require the SPSS Advanced Module.

A language school is trying out two new teaching techniques in its classroom. Our dependent variable is each student's test score taken at the end of the course unit under one or other of the teaching techniques. The design is within-subjects as each student is taught in all three ways. It is between-subjects in that half the students are adults and half are adolescents. (This design is also referred to as 'split plot', reflecting its origins in agricultural research.)

Input process

The design structure can be represented like this:

Table 10.6

	Usual teaching	Test 1	Test 2
Adults			
Adolescents			

In Variable View, we require three adjacent rows to represent the three conditions to be undertaken by all the participants. Another row is required for the grouping variable.

Image 10.17

	Name	Type	Width	Decimals	Label	Values
1	Case	Numeric	8	0	Student number	None
2	Category	Numeric	8	0	Age category	{1, Adults}...
3	Usual	Numeric	8	0	Usual method	None
4	Test1	Numeric	8	0	Test method 1	None
5	Test2	Numeric	8	0	Test method 2	None

The age category 'Measure' should be set to 'Nominal' and it requires values: I have used 1 = Adults and 2 = Adolescents.

Image 10.18

	Case	Category	Usual	Test1	Test2
1	1	Adults	80	82	78
2	2	Adults	65	67	64
3	3	Adults	50	58	45
4	4	Adults	68	69	70
5	5	Adults	63	66	63
6	6	Adults	57	56	58
7	7	Adolescents	84	83	84
8	8	Adolescents	70	75	71
9	9	Adolescents	70	76	72
10	10	Adolescents	57	62	58
11	11	Adolescents	46	60	42
12	12	Adolescents	55	64	51

And here is our data in Data View.

Analysis

To check for extreme values, *Analyze/Descriptive Statistics/Explore* would be useful.

Select *Analyze/General Linear Model/Repeated Measures.* In Within-subject Factor Name, replace 'factor1' with an overall variable name such as 'tests' (no more than eight letters, lower case and not the same word as any of the variable names already chosen). The number of levels for tests will be 3. Click 'Add', which should place 'tests(3)' in the main box. In the Measure Name box, write in a name for your dependent variable such as 'score' and click 'Add' again.

Image 10.19

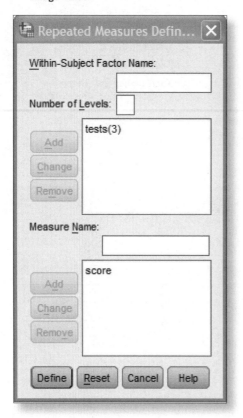

Then press 'Define'.

Transfer Usual, Test1 and Test2 to the Within-Subjects Variables box in the Repeated Measures dialog box. 'Category' goes into the Between-subjects Factor box.

Image 10.20

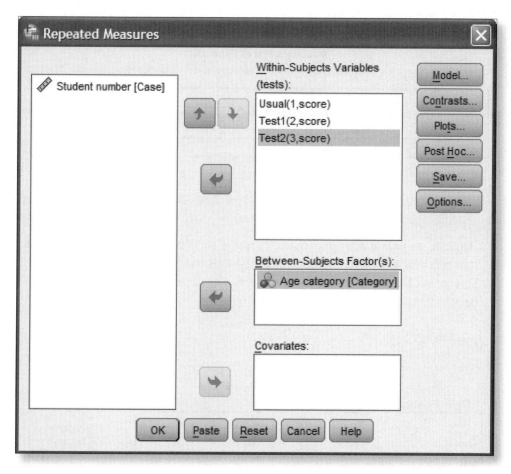

Go into 'Plots', putting 'tests' in 'Horizontal Axis' as it has the most levels and Category into 'Separate Lines' and click 'Add' to put tests*Category into the field at the bottom. Press 'Continue'.

Go to 'Options' and choose the following options: Place 'tests' in the 'Display Means for' box. Tick 'Compare main effects' and select 'Sidak' for 'Confidence interval adjustment'. Select 'Descriptive statistics' and 'Estimates of effect size'. Click 'Continue'.

We do not need 'Post Hoc' tests for the between-subjects category (Age Category), as there are only two levels. Had there been more, then the Tukey check box would have been selected to examine the levels in pairs. Click 'Continue' and then 'OK'.

Image 10.21

Mauchly's Test of Sphericity[b]

Measure: MEASURE_1

			Epsilon[a]		
Within Subjects Effect	Mauchly's W	Sig.	Greenhouse-Geisser	Huynh-Feldt	Lower-bound
tests	.161	.000	.544	.620	.500

Houston, we have a problem. Mauchly's test is significant, in a pronounced way, so the sphericity assumption for repeated measures has been well and truly violated. This means that we will need to consider reading adjusted values. We will come back to this (edited) output box very shortly.

Image 10.22

Tests of Within-Subjects Effects

Measure:score

Source		Mean Square	F	Sig	Partial Eta Squared
test	Sphericity Assumed	93.528	8.988	.002	.473
	Greenhouse-Geisser	172.036	8.988	0.11	.473
	Huynh-Feldt	150.907	8.988	.008	.473
	Lower-bound	187.056	8.988	0.13	.473
test * categories	Sphericity Assumed	14.083	1.353	.281	.119
	Greenhouse-Geisser	25.905	1.353	.274	.119
	Huynh-Feldt	22.723	1.353	.277	.119
	Lower-bound	28.167	1.353	.272	.119
Error(tests)	Sphericity Assumed	10.406			
	Greenhouse-Geisser	19.140			
	Huynh-Feldt	16.789			
	Lower-bound	20.811			

We can no longer read from the 'Sphericity Assumed' line, but need to select an adjustment. Some experts always use Huynh–Feldt, others always Greenhouse–Geisser. My advice is to go back to the Mauchly's Test of Sphericity output box. If the Epsilon for Huynh–Feldt is greater than .75, use Huynh–Feldt; otherwise use Greenhouse–Geisser. In this case, the Epsilon value is .620, so we should use Greenhouse–Geisser. This being the case, when we return to the output for effects, our 'tests' variable is .011 (p < .02), rather than the lower critical value of the usual reading.

We don't have to worry about the interaction, as this is clearly not significant.

In the 'Tests of Between-subjects Effects', we find that the effect for age category is also non-significant.

The 'Estimated Means' tells us that the second test result is stronger than the others.

Image 10.23

Pairwise Comparisons

Measure: score

(I) retake	(J) retake	Mean Difference (I-J)	Std. Error	Sig.[b]	95% Confidence Interval for Difference[b]	
					Lower Bound	Upper Bound
1	2	-4.417*	1.186	.012	-7.809	-1.024
	3	.750	.743	.708	-1.374	2.874
2	1	4.417*	1.186	.012	1.024	7.809
	3	5.167*	1.801	.049	.015	10.318
3	1	-.750	.743	.708	-2.874	1.374
	2	-5.167*	1.801	.049	-10.318	-.015

Based on estimated marginal means
* The mean difference is significant at the .05 level.
b. Adjustement for multiple comparisons: Sidak.

The Pairwise Comparisons output, according to the Sidak adjustment, indicates that the first and second conditions are significantly different at p value .012, p < .02, similarly the second and third conditions at .049, p < .05.

If you use the Bonferroni adjustment, however, the relationship between the third and first condition is .050, which is not smaller than .05.

You will find a detailed discussion shortly in the statistical theory box about possible choices of adjustment tests. For the moment, we can say that while many use the Bonferroni as the traditional default, Bonferroni is nowadays considered too harsh (Rice, 1989) and the Sidak option has been the default in this book.

In this case, I would point out that we already know that this particular set of data has seriously violated an assumption for repeated measures tests and I am inclined to think that a more conservative test is more appropriate. However, given the closeness to significance, it may well be worth citing both tests and suggesting that a replication would be worthwhile. Apart from anything else, if readers are given both sets of readings, they can come to their own conclusions.

Mixed design three-way ANOVA −2 within-subjects and 1 between-subjects

Mixed designs require the SPSS Advanced Module.

Using our previous example, we may choose to have two teachers trying out the methods in order to get some idea of whether or not teacher idiosyncrasy is at play. So we now have two within-subject variables, test and teacher. In addition to the variables 'Case' and 'Age Category', we have to enter six new variables into Variable View, combining the method and the teacher. This is the structure within Data View (using imaginary figures):

Table 10.7

Case	Category	UsualT1	UsualT2	Test1T1	Test1T2	Test2T1	Test2T2
12	Adults	80	83	86	88	81	82

Select *Analyze/General Linear Model/Repeated Measures.*

In Within-subject Factor Name, replace factor1 with 'tests', with 3 for the number of levels. Then click 'Add'. As in the Two-Way ANOVA Repeated Measures, you need to 'define' twice. Do the same with 'teachers' but with only 2 for levels.

Transfer UsualT1, UsualT2, Test1T1, Test1T2, Test2T1 and Test2T2 to the Within-Subjects Variables box in the Repeated Measures dialog box. Be very careful with the sequence. Make sure that 'Within-subjects Variables' at the top of the dialog box says [test, teacher] and that your transfer to the right-hand box goes:

UsualT1[1,1,score]
UsualT2[1,2,score]
Test1T1[2,1,score]
Test1T2[2,2,score]
Test2T1[3,1,score]
Test2T2[3,2,score]

so that your entries mirror the data entry in Data View. Then, as with the Mixed Design two-way ANOVA, Age Category goes in the Between-subjects Factor box.

Mixed design three-way ANOVA – 2 between-subjects and 1 within-subjects

Mixed designs require the SPSS Advanced Module.

This time, we'll have a different variant of our language school tests. Let's say that we decide to look at whether or not the tests affect males and females differently. So we have tests as the within-subjects variable and both age category and gender as the between-subjects variables.

In Variable View, we would want the following variables: Case, Gender, Age, Usual, Test1, Test2. Values need to be assigned to the gender grouping variable as well as to 'age'.

In this variant, when you get to the Repeated Measures dialog box, there will only be one variable at the top as the Within-subjects Variable: 'tests'. Usual, Test1 and Test2 will be transferred to the right-hand window. However, two variables will be transferred to the Between-subjects Factor at the bottom, Age Category and Gender.

Statistical theory – one more for the gipper

Omnibus tests

If we want to examine the differences between more than two conditions, we could use tests such as the t test again and again. However, this multiple usage increases our chances of creating Type 1 errors, where apparently significant results are, in fact, flukes. Another option would be to alter the significance level, say from $p < .05$ to $p < .01$ – this rather crude solution is very likely to create Type 2 errors, where we miss significant results. Omnibus tests, such as Friedman, Kruskal–Wallis and ANOVA, are methods of examining significance overall.

Analysis of variance

An economic and elegant alternative to multiple t tests (Parker, 1979), ANOVA calculates how much variance comes from independent variables and how much is due to error (error variance). The proportion comprising the variable's variance divided by the error is called the F ratio ('F' in SPSS output). The more the variable's effect outweighs the error, the bigger the F ratio and the more likely that the effect is a significant one.

Within-subjects (related) ANOVA includes a variance estimate relating to the subjects.

The null hypothesis tested by the ANOVA is that means of the data groups are all equal. The ANOVA test is an 'omnibus test', examining only overall effects.

Multiple comparisons

It is possible to examine the differences between individual conditions (levels) of variables by running a series of t tests, but the more tests that are run, the greater the likelihood of Type 1 error (assuming significance when the null hypothesis should be accepted).

There is little opposition to the idea of *planned tests.* If you have a theoretical reason to believe, before data is collected, that certain variable pairings are likely to be important, then you will want to test them for significance as well as the overall effects. t tests or the LSD (least square difference) option provided by SPSS for ANOVA are generally considered reasonable in such cases.

Post hoc tests, conducted in an unplanned way with or after the ANOVA, are highly controversial (Games, 1971; Sato, 1996). Before the widespread use of personal computers, many social scientists conducted statistical tests by hand and ANOVA calculations in textbooks were not always accompanied by post hoc tests (for example,

Greene and D'Oliveira, 1982), giving the impression that no such tests were available. Apart from the comparative difficulties of performing these by hand, there was a fair amount of criticism of the usefulness of such tests (Nelder, 1971; Plackett, 1971; Preece, 1982), leading to the impression that only the overall result could be accepted, a position defended by the great statistician R.A. Fisher (1935). Many researchers before the advent of widespread computer usage tended not to use them (Parker, 1979). It was argued by Nelder (1999) that "multiple comparison methods have no place at all in the interpretation of data".

Another opinion is that multiple comparisons are over-used, partly because of an unwillingness to specify contrasts and partly because of the availability of software which produces them as a matter of course (Pearce, 1993). While unplanned tests are generally considered to be less powerful than planned tests (Day and Quinn, 1989), I would at least consider an intermediate view. While their results should be interpreted with considerable scepticism, post hoc tests may assist in suggesting new hypotheses for investigation. (Hess and Olejnik, 1997, put forward yet another view; that ANOVA tests should be abandoned for most purposes in favour of focused hypothesis testing.)

Let us assume that we wish to continue using ANOVA and *post hoc* testing. Some researchers believe that post hoc tests should only be made after significance is found in the ANOVA main effect or interaction, considering any other testing of internal information to be dredging (for example Wyseure, 2003). Other researchers (for example, Huck, 2009) are quite sure that this is a misconception and that post hoc tests may be used regardless of a non-significant main effect.

On the whole, post hoc tests are commonly used and analysed. In order to reduce the likelihood of Type 1 error arising from using multiple t tests, specialist tests are used which make adjustments to take into account the likely effect of multiple comparisons. Although I provide some suggested ways of using post hoc tests, there is no definitive formulation; this is a controversial topic and you should always report your use of post hoc tests and how you used them.

Assuming that we do wish to use them, here are a few of the strategies suggested by various commentators. As you develop your work with statistics, you may develop your own opinion on which (if any) of these make the most sense.

The strategies tend to be based upon just how strict or otherwise the available tests are. Conservative tests are somewhat more likely to make a Type 2 error (rejecting a significant result), while 'liberal' ones may conceivably succumb to Type 1 (accepting a result when the null hypothesis should be accepted).

Within-subjects tests

While several other texts still use the Bonferroni test as the default option (for example, Kinnear and Gray, 2004), it is these days considered rather harsh (Rice, 1989). The default in this book is to use the Sidak. On the other hand, when I had serious doubts about the data, I felt that it would be sensible to use the more conservative Bonferroni but to allow the reader to come to their own judgement by reporting both results. In many cases, though, including several in this book, the results of the two tests do not differ greatly.

Another strategy is to use both tests when examining relatively few pairings and report the lowest result. I personally think that if you use two you should report both.

The real problem comes when reporting large numbers of pairings; in my opinion the best way to avoid this is to restrict pairing analyses to smallish numbers based on reasonable theoretical grounds rather than trawling for unexpected results.
As we have discussed in previous chapters, there are data reduction methods available.

Between-subjects tests

When dealing with between-subjects pairings, the Scheffe and the Bonferroni are generally considered to be the most conservative. Then comes the Tukey. The Dunnet is considered more liberal, then the Duncan, with LSD (least square difference) being the most liberal. (Dallal, 2001).

One strategy is to use a combination of Tukey and Fisher's LSD (Dallal, 2001, whose web page makes very interesting reading on the subject of multiple comparisons). If Tukey deems a result to be significant, accept it as significant. If LSD considers it to be non-significant (and remember that LSD is a very liberal test), then consider the result to be non-significant. If LSD considers the result significant, but Tukey does not, consider the differences as being open to further investigation. (Maybe try to replicate your results with fresh data.)

Test only the conditions you think are important. Use the Tukey if they are all important (Dallal, 2001.)

Use Tukey for larger numbers of conditions and Bonferroni for smaller numbers (Field, 2009).

Use the Bonferroni (and maybe also Scheffe) if unplanned, as a conservative anti–dredging device, and the Tukey if planned (Kleinbaum et al, 2008).

Use a batch of tests and pick the one offering the lowest critical value (Howell, 2011).

The Tukey test is the most widely used (Tsoumakas et al, 2005). The default in this book has been to test all of the conditions – having limited the number of original ANOVA variables to those which are meaningful – and to use Tukey.

Effect discovery versus treatment choice strategy for multiple comparisons
The authors of a rather useful internet article (Hilton and Armstrong, 2006) suggest that 'In many circumstances, different *post hoc* tests may lead to the same conclusions and which of the tests is actually used is often a matter of fashion or personal taste. However, each test addresses the statistical problems in a unique way.' They suggest that one useful strategy is to base your test use on the purpose of the investigation. Where we would wish to be as sure as possible as to whether or not a treatment has an effect, then we would opt for a conservative test. When choosing between different treatments, a liberal test would be less likely to miss an effect.

Choices according to data set types
You will also find a set of recommendations for different post hoc tests according to different types of data set on a website article (SSTARS, 2011). This one takes some reading, however. If you can get your head round it, you will really have come a long way.

Notes on ANCOVA (analysis of covariance)

In the chapter on correlations and regression, Chapter 9, we looked briefly at partialling out, or controlling for, a variable which was closely related to the variables being studied. A covariate is a variable which has a linear relationship with the dependent variable. This effect often leads to a Type 2 error when examining a pre- and post-test study using the usual methods such as *t* tests: because of the strength of the relationship between pre–test and post–test attributes, an apparently non-significant result may, in fact, be a false negative.

When discussing the two-factor between-subjects ANOVA, we also noted the existence of a 'Covariates box' which could be used. This brings us to ANCOVA.

ANCOVA can be used to partial out more variables than the partialling out procedure previously discussed.

ANCOVA has also been used to try to remove the effects of fixed groups (for example, secretaries, managers and manual staff) from a more general effect being studied.

The idea in both cases is to remove statistical noise. Typical covariates are IQ (these days, results of specific psychometric tests) and age. If we take age as an example, it may perhaps correlate with a motivational measure, or make a difference between fixed groups, for example, graduate trainees and experienced practitioners, affecting the interpretation of the results of a training course. As we may not have the time or inclination to create groups of people all of the same age or IQ, let alone several groups with different ages or IQ measurements, then we may wish to statistically reduce the influence of the covariate.

But before you go rushing off to use the covariate box on an ANOVA dialog box, I wish to raise some serious methodological issues which I hope will make you think again.

Statistical assumptions for ANCOVA

There are a range of statistical assumptions necessary for using ANCOVA. First, there are the same assumptions as for ANOVA and other parametric tests: interval data, normal distribution and (where the number of subjects in each condition is different) homogeneity of variance. In the case of within-subjects (repeated measures) experiments, sphericity is considered important in measuring the relationships between the variables.

Then there are additional assumptions relating to ANCOVA. One, unsurprisingly, is that the covariate needs to correlate with the dependent variable in a linear way; the stronger the relationship, the more useful ANCOVA will be. A scatter plot is appropriate for looking at this.

At the same time, the variable and covariate must not be over-correlated. We examine this by looking at the regression lines for the covariate across the different groups; these need to run in parallel, neither crossing nor too close to each other. This 'homogeneity of regression', which can also be checked with scatter plots, is arguably the most important of the assumptions.

The covariate should be unrelated to the independent variable. This should be checked at the design stage.

If there is more than one covariate, the covariates should not be over correlated with each other. This may be checked by scatter plots and correlations.

Problems with using ANCOVA

The above statistical assumptions indicate that you need a very narrowly defined data set to run an ANCOVA. While the proponents of ANOVA and other parametric tests refer to the robustness of these tests, there is some evidence which indicates that the ANCOVA is rather less than robust. Any unreliability in the data is likely to produce distortions which make interpretation difficult and even downright misleading.

I would also suggest that you are unlikely to come across data which warrants this treatment. In this book, non-parametric tests have preceded parametric tests in recognition of their usability with a wider range of data sets. When we get to ANCOVA the restrictions become even less applicable. It is also argued that the requirement for group controls of fairly similar regression slopes may render statistical control rather unnecessary.

Even when the data is correctly used, inference is difficult. I would suggest (with respect) that this is for advanced users of statistical tests. And maybe not even then; in its time ANCOVA has claimed some very high profile victims (see Campbell, 1989, on the dangers of using ANCOVA).

For those interested in ANCOVA, various internet articles should scratch the itch (for example, Furman University, 2007).

Some alternatives to ANCOVA

If the assumptions are not met, or I have put you off sufficiently, various alternatives are possible. I will suggest the most accessible ones.

You can still perform the ANOVA or t test without the covariate, merely accepting that the results are not as accurate as you would like and recording the likely existence of the mediating factor. Another idea, if numbers are sufficient, is stratification: breaking up the statistics according to groupings of different levels of the covariate (for example, intelligence bandings), using the categories as 'fixed factors'. Another option is to use multiple regression to re-examine your model. Here, instead of performing the standard version of regression, you would use hierarchical (sequential) regression, selecting 'stepwise' in the SPSS 'method' box.

Table 10.8

Test	Details
Within subjects factorial ANOVA	Same subjects only, two or more factors
Between subjects factorial ANOVA	Different subjects only, two or more factors
Mixed design factorial ANOVA	Same *and* different subjects, two or more factors

Talking point

Our discussions of post hoc tests and of the use of ANCOVA raise some points about our mental habits, both within research and, I would suggest, in real life. One is the adoption of technology not on its merits but because we can. Another is the use of software that is referred to as 'powerful', especially when we are not told in what way such a thing is powerful (ok, in the case of tests, it means more likely to find an effect). There is also a tendency to see complexity as a virtue, or perhaps to see simplicity as naivety. Yet a further one is to choose ways of thinking because of perceived popularity or the example of respected users. (I shall now make you happier by going to live in a cave.)

Chapter 11

The time until events: survival analysis

Part Two

The set of tests from this area of statistics requires the SPSS Advanced Module.

Survival analysis is concerned with how long it takes for an outcome, or **event**, to take place. It focuses on the interval between the starting point – for example, the completion of a course of treatment – and the event; this interval is known as the **survival time, observation period** or **follow-up period.**

Traditionally, the events of interest have been the deaths of patients after a therapeutic intervention, hence the term 'survival analysis', but this range of techniques can be used much more widely. We can look at many other outcomes, positive and negative, such as employees resigning after the completion of a reorganisation initiative, staff promotions after a training course, or the consequences of changes in taxation laws on such events as students graduating, university drop-outs and couples being married.

We are interested in learning about the survival time. Do events tend to accelerate after a particular period of time? Are there phases during which events tend to cluster? What proportion of individuals are affected in a particular phase?

It is also possible that we may wish to contrast different samples. Does the group on a special training programme truly have a different promotion rate from a control group on a traditional course? Will drop-out rates for an employment rehabilitation scheme differ according to different levels of support?

Other ways of measuring event rates could be considered, for example, the graphical representation of averages or using the predictive power of linear regression. Survival analysis, however, has a range of advantages. It provides a far more informative analysis of the process under investigation. Non-linear patterns are not a problem; note, for example, that if you are looking at mortality, then there will inevitably be sizeable shifts from the average at both the beginning and the end of the follow-up period. Crucially, however, survival analysis accounts for missing information, known as **censored events**.

Censored information is that which the researcher can only guess at. This includes cases where the event fails to occur until after the follow-up period has expired; the fact, for example, that a cancer sufferer does not die within the survival time does not mean that he may not die from cancer after observations have been concluded. Similarly, individuals who have withdrawn from the study or with whom researchers have lost contact (**loss to follow-up**), may or may not experience the pertinent event. Even when we are certain that events will have taken place (we are all dead in the long run, said Keynes), we can not assume that we know *when*.

If we omit censored data, or count it as having the same duration as the latest recorded event, then we underestimate the effect under investigation. Although we could negate the time distortions by just focusing on events, we would lose the considerable richness of data provided by looking at duration.

Survival analysis measures the occurrence of events in terms of the duration of time in which they take place. It also takes into account censored data. This is the case when data is missing during or after the monitoring period; both of these are called 'right censored data'. You should avoid introducing 'left censored data', where complications precede the survival time; some procedures can be put in place to deal with this, but we can't be dealing with it here (you could try Klein and Moeschberger, 2003).

Some assumptions about the data are required by survival analysis. Continuous data is required; this is usually days in the case of the Kaplan–Meier survival function. Longer gaps such as years should be measured by life tables. Each record must be a different one; that is, you don't include the same person more than once. Censoring should be random; you must not exclude individuals from the survival period because they seem to be a particularly high (or low) risk. The event should be categorical; either they're dead or they're alive, cured or not, promoted or not, lapsed or not.

Time is the predictor variable. Status is the criterion variable.

The Kaplan–Meier survival function

This requires the SPSS Advanced Module.

The beauty of the Kaplan–Meier is the intuitiveness of the survival plot. Its steepness shows whether or not the probability of an event – for example, promotion – is high or low, whether or not this accelerates or decelerates over time and differences between groups of patients under different conditions.

Input process

The minimum requirements are two variables. One, a scale measure, represents the 'survival time' (follow-up time), as represented by days or hours. The other, a nominal measure, represents either the event or censorship (loss to follow-up). I would suggest providing a '1' for the event and a '0' for censored data. So each time represents either the event (death, graduation and so on) or a withdrawal from the study.

It is also quite common to provide a grouping variable, a 'nominal' measure, so that performances can be compared.

Analysis

Exercise 1

Image 11.1

	Days	Promotions
1	40	Promotion
2	60	Promotion
3	62	Promotion
4	80	Promotion
5	85	Promotion
6	108	Promotion
7	108	Promotion
8	115	Censored
9	140	Promotion
10	160	Censored
11	180	Censored
12	180	Censored

Let us start with a very simple example. A management course has been completed among a group of staff at a similar level; the study lasts for 180 days and focuses on subsequent promotions. The cohort is deliberately small here, as we are interested in introducing this form of analysis rather than concerning ourselves with statistical significance or organisational meaningfulness.

In terms of *Variable View*, 'Days' and 'Promotions' are the variables to be created. Promotions is a nominal variable, with the values 0 for 'Censored' and 1 for 'Promotion'. The numerical data is entered into *Data View* as above.

Select *Analyze/Survival/Kaplan–Meier*. Transfer 'Days' to the 'Time' field on the right. Transfer 'Promotions' to the 'Status' field. Underneath the Status box, press Define Event. Keep to 'Single value' and enter the number 1. (Don't worry about the zero, as SPSS takes this to be the censored event.) Click 'Continue'.

Back at the Kaplan–Meier dialog box, press 'Options'. Select 'survival tables', 'mean and median survival' and, from the plots submenu, 'survival' (we will deal with 'hazard' in the second exercise). Click 'Continue' and, in the main dialog box, click 'OK'.

We now consider the output. The initial summary data reading tells us that we have input the data correctly (8 events, 4 censored). The survival table tells us the story in numerical form:

The first promotion takes place on the fortieth day. Subsequent promotions take place until day 108, when two people are promoted. Day 115 contains censored data; perhaps somebody left the organisation. We then get another promotion and another piece of censored data on day 160. The remaining two members of the cohort are not promoted by the last day of observation, day 180, so they become censored data.

Statistically speaking, the survival table repeats our input with two important additions: The number of cumulative events, which omits censored data, and the 'Estimate' column which gives us the proportion of the cohort still unaffected by events after a period of time (for example, almost 92% after 40 days and about 31% after 140 days). Initially, this is worked out simply by dividing the number of unaffected cases by the total; however, after the first censored event, the Kaplan–Meier adjusts the figure to an estimate to take into account censored data.

We are then provided with the mean and median survival times. When we have larger data sets, the Confidence Intervals will become more important, so we will return to these in the next exercise.

Image 11.2

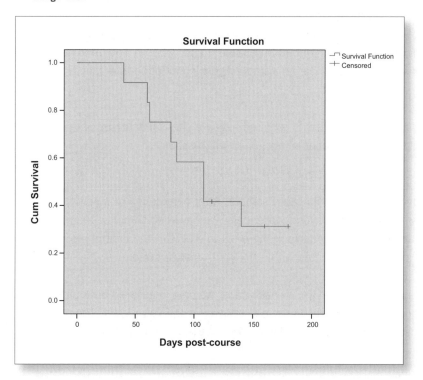

Events on the survival function chart are marked by a short drop, usually of the same depth, but you can see a bigger drop at day 108 when two events happened. Censored data are marked by a cross but, as you see, do not affect the survival function's shape.

Kaplan–Meier takes censored data into account in making calculations but makes no assumptions about the effect, the rate of promotions.

The calculations of the likelihood of an event happening have been worked out on the plot. Note that the upright, or y axis, referred to as 'cumulative survival' runs from 0 to 1, from zero to 100% of the individuals in the study. At 1, we have 100% of our cohort unaffected. After the first event, after 40 days, it looks like a little over 90% of the cohort is unaffected. If you return to the survival table, you will find that this is .917. If we call it 92%, then we can say that the probability of promotion after 40 days is approximately 8% (100%–92%). Note that in real life, we would not make such extrapolations so early with such a small sample.

Then we look at the middle of the upright (y) axis and then across to the intercept (where an imaginary horizontal line would meet the function line), the x axis value is the estimated median survival time, 108 days. Do note, however, that the median is indeed an estimate and, when it comes to serious consideration of the data (in larger samples), the confidence intervals are very important.

The above procedure is all that is required to run a survival analysis, but you can also do a comparison with another group, as will be seen.

Exercise 2

Now we move to a more complicated sample. After completion of a new rehabilitation programme for young offenders, we have two samples: members of the experimental group undertook the programme, with the control group undergoing standard procedures within the youth justice system.

The follow-up period is 90 days. In each case, we have measured days until the event, the occurrence of a fresh criminal offence, or the last record. The censored data comprises where the young people have withdrawn from the programme or are otherwise 'lost to follow-up'.

In Variable View, you will need to create a 'days' variable, a status variable (values 1 for offending and 0 for censored data) and a group variable (1 for the experimental group and 2 for the control group).

You will need to enter the data below in the following fashion in Data View: the number goes in the days column; the default in the status variable is a 1, except where I have inserted a zero, which represents censored data; your grouping variable column will have a 1 for the experimental group and a 2 for the control group.

Experimental group (15 participants):

27, 29 (0), 40, 54, 60, 72, 83, 84, 88, 90 (0), 90 (0), 90 (0), 90 (0), 90 (0), 90 (0).

Control group (15 participants):

16, 17, 18, 20, 22, 25, 25, 30 (0), 53, 71, 84, 86, 90 (0), 90 (0), 90 (0).

For the moment, we want to analyse the whole sample, so do not do anything with the grouping variable. You should run the procedure as you did before, but within the Options dialog, additionally select the Hazard plot.

Among other things, you will get a great big survival table. The basic story, as represented by the data, is that offences start to occur in the control group after the first two weeks following the rehabilitation course. By the end of the month, two individuals have either withdrawn from the programme or are otherwise lost to follow-up. As the weeks go by, some more offences occur in both groups. By the end of the 90 day period, 6 members of the experimental group survive the observation period without offending (note that the Kaplan–Meier, during the calculations, does not ignore the possibility of a future offence). Three members of the control group also survive the follow-up period without offending.

One thing to note is the number of censored events at the end of the row of figures. In general, a high number of these can mean that a lot of individuals do indeed fail to experience the event in question; but an alternative explanation may be that the follow-up period is just not long enough to make sufficient observations. We can say, however, that there is a 51% survival likelihood after 72 days (49% are likely to relapse by then).

On the other hand, 33% are likely to continue without offending up to or beyond 90 days.

The table is followed by the means and medians. While the mean survival time is 64 days, the confidence intervals say that values will typically fall between about 54 and 74 days. Citing confidence intervals can here be seen as rather useful for predicting. Do note that we also cite in reports the median survival time, here 83 days, with confidence intervals of about 66 and 99 days.

The role of the confidence intervals should become clearer to you when you examine the survival function. Considering the mean's confidence intervals first, you will see that an awful lot happens between that period of 54 and 74 days. The median as a statistic of central tendency shows something different, the central values; the confidence intervals show us a considerable flurry of activity between those 66 and 99 days. The median is generally considered to be the more useful statistic in survival analysis and, as you see, the confidence intervals are highly informative.

Image 11.3

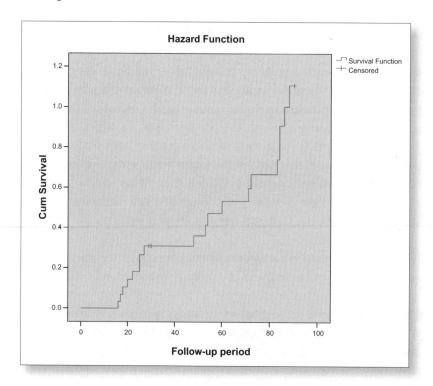

The hazard plot shows the relative acceleration of risk, the y axis representing 'cumulative hazard'. It indicates a steep trend of re-offending in the third week, with a fairly pronounced trend towards the end of the follow-up period.

Please ensure that you have saved your data.

Exercise 3

Using the same sample as in the previous exercise, let us now contrast the two groups. Please return to *Analyze/Survival/Kaplan–Meier* and this time transfer the grouping variable into the 'Factor' slot. (You would use 'Strata' if you had different conditions to contrast, for example, with and without drug problems, which would require another variable.) Also, press 'Compare Factor', selecting all three test statistics: Log Rank, Breslow and Tarone–Ware.

The survival table appears as two sub-boxes, devoted to each of the two groups. We note at the bottom of each division the number of people who have lasted up to or beyond the 90-day observation period: 6 in the experimental group and 3 in the control group. There are also clear differences between the groups in the rest of the survival data. Little more than 50% of the control group is likely to survive without offending after 30 days, while in the same period there is very little movement among the experimental group. By the end of follow-up, only 23% of the controls are likely to survive without incident (77% re-offending likelihood), compared to 43% of the experimental group. The means and medians tell a similar story (note that the median survival time is generally deemed to be of more use in survival analysis than the mean), although the smaller sub-samples make the confidence intervals somewhat less informative overall.

Tests of significance in survival analysis

Before seeing whether or not the differences in our example are significant, we need to consider the tests of significance offered by SPSS.

The Log Rank test is best when testing a survival curve throughout its entire course and is more sensitive when the two groups show consistently similar patterns.

The Breslow test is considered to be more sensitive to differences between groups at early stages. (This test can, however, tend towards Type Two errors judging results not to be significant when they are – a 'False Negative'; the opposite is the Type One error, a 'False Positive', seeing significance when it should be absent.)

The Tarone–Ware test is preferred where survival curves intersect or move away from each other.

When we look at the survival functions and consider the descriptions above, the Breslow test is the most appropriate in this situation. It indicates significant between-group differences with a p value of .029, giving a critical value of $p < .05$.

(If we look for interest's sake at the less appropriate tests, the differences appear, unsurprisingly, to be insignificant under the Log Rank test (.083). This reflects the differences between the patterns of the two groups. Tarone–Ware, however, shows $p < .05$ which illustrates the potential dangers of dredging.)

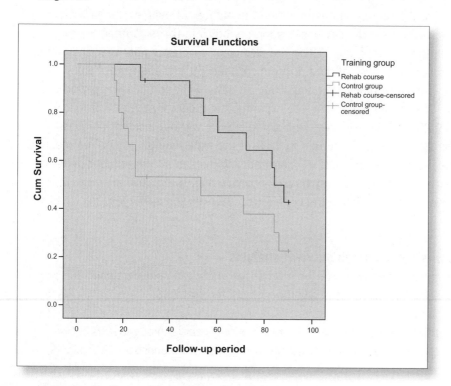

The survival plot tells an interesting story. The control group, on the lower line, re-offend very quickly, within about a week. If this is usual criminologically, then fine, it shows that the new rehabilitation scheme would appear to help participants to avoid this slough; it would be worth checking, however, in case something unusual affected this particular group of young people at this time. There would appear to be a clear difference between the groups over time, although there is a similar decline towards the end, which does rather suggest that the observation time should have been somewhat longer.

Image 11.5

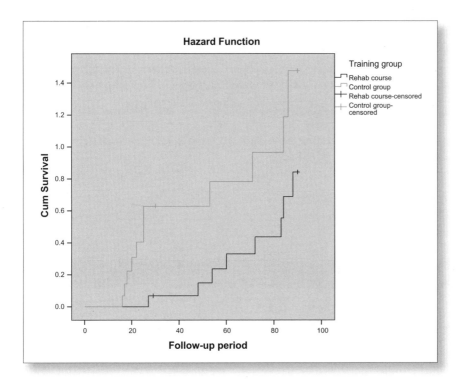

The hazard plot shows a clear increase in risk among the control group in the early period. Increased risk appears at the end for both groups. At the very least, we should be concerned about the possible vulnerability of all young ex-offenders during this second period of time. (Reminder: this was a fictional study.)

Please keep your file for use in the next exercise.

The life table

This requires the SPSS Advanced Module.

Generally speaking, if you can use the Kaplan–Meier, with its richness of data, you should. However, in spite of it being a non-parametric method, the Kaplan–Meier is designed to look at continuous data. If we are looking at intervals, such as months, quarters and years, then a life table should be considered. As in the

Kaplan–Meier, the risk is adjusted to take account of losses to follow-up. The minimum sample size for a life table, in terms of the number of participants starting the study, should be at least 30, although some authorities recommend at least 100. Life tables are typically used with samples of thousands.

One example of its usage would be if we were interested in how long convicted drink-drivers remain out of trouble after regaining their licences.

However, to save space, we will use the data from the previous exercise on Kaplan–Meier.

Select *Analyze/Survival/Life Tables.*

Image 11.6

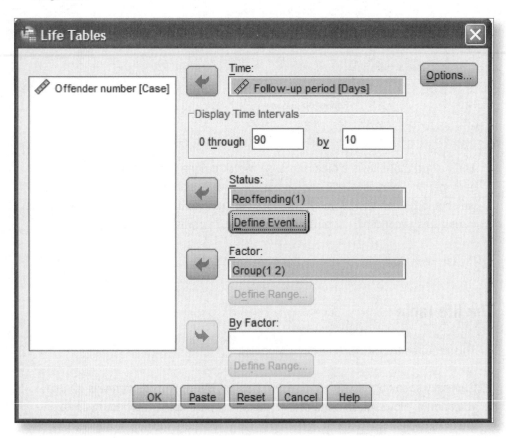

The first time slot of course contains the Days variable. The 'Display Time Intervals' slots both need to be completed. The first slot shows that I have chosen to cover the data from 0 to 90 days, the second that I have chosen to have a rather more compact analysis by looking at the data in 10-day chunks.

Assuming the Status variable has been called 'Reoffending', you can see that when operating 'Define Range', I have chosen the single value option and entered 1 as the event (the committing of a new offence).

Although I have shown the Factor slot in this image to show how it would look, I would not normally compare group variables with such a small sample when using life tables. The method used was to transfer the 'Group' variable to the slot and then, in 'Define Range', to enter 1 and 2 as the groups of interest.

The results will be very similar to the Kaplan–Meier, but lacking features such as the statistical tests of group differences and confidence intervals.

This table of survival analysis techniques only refers to tests used in this chapter.

N.B. Non-parametric tests can be used with 'parametric' data.

Table 11.1

Test	Data	Purpose
Kaplan–Meier	Non-parametric. Large and small sample. Data must be continuous (that is, not less frequent than days).	Tracking events over time.
Life Table	Non-parametric. Large samples. Interval data (for example months, quarters, years).	Tracking events over time.
Log Rank, Breslow and Tarone–Ware tests	Non-parametric. For differences in usage, see earlier notes in this chapter.	Significance of Kaplan–Meier group differences.

You will find that SPSS also offers Cox's regression as a type of survival analysis. Also known as the Cox model, this provides survival analysis with a multiple regression technique, allowing different independent variables to be weighted. This is semi-parametric, requiring certain assumptions to be met about the data. I feel that this and methods of analysis such as logit and probit are not appropriate for an introductory text.

Talking point

The statistical methods referred to in this chapter are often referred to by the overall title of Survival Analysis. This reflects its most familiar usage in health statistics, the tracking of the survival rate of patients over time; this is made manifest in SPSS's use of 'terminal events' in its survival tables. Having said that, I feel that it is more useful to consider it as the study of the time until events, as we are not necessarily discussing life and death and may be measuring events which are positive and not necessarily dramatic.

Whatever we call it, it is one of the oldest fields of statistics, going back to actuarial tables in the seventeenth century. As with many disciplines its study was later stimulated by warfare; people wanted to carry out reliability analysis to see how long it took for a weapon to fail. Within engineering reliability analysis is also called reliability theory, which begins to tell us why survival analysis has not yet featured in general statistical introductions by other authors (cf Davis, 2010).

Different names for this set of techniques appear in different disciplines. One such term that I prefer for its broad applicability is 'time to event analysis'. Names such as duration analysis, duration modelling and event history analysis proliferate in economics and sociology. Another term, in historic sociology, is event structure analysis (ESA). Studies in economics and sociology are often longitudinal, comprising survey follow-ups which record the time until different life events. These frequently relate to employment status and personal life events respectively.

In the spheres of medicine and nursing survival analysis is often to be taken literally, and there has been a proliferation of studies about mortality or the onset of illness. The medical connotation has led to the term survival analysis taking hold, along with an assumption that this is primarily part of a medical paradigm.

We therefore have a paradox. The varied nomenclature produces an impression of specialisation; the specialisation is so widespread as to be a commonplace.

As demonstrated, the techniques are highly versatile. While they may offer less predictive value than finely honed linear techniques, they apply to real-life problems. As Perrigot et al (2004) explain in their highly readable article, many organisational failures are not subject to linear trends but are, in fact, a history of disasters. Their article takes the example of the study of business franchises, the survival of which can be studied by comparing the progress of franchises of different sizes, ownership category, urbanisation or guiding policies. Clearly, such analyses could be applied to other organisations, networks and projects. The authors suggest that the techniques could be used for the analysis of the stability of international joint ventures and the prediction of illegal corporate behaviour.

You could also study car crashes or incidents of violence. Categories for contrast could be the implementation of different safety or policing devices, and controls where no such device is in place. One contrast often used in medical studies is between urban and rural settings. Kahneman (2011), however, points out the dangers of this: large swings can be more apparent than real in small data sets, so some apparent differences in rural studies can represent the random fluctuations of a few dice throws.

However! Be of good cheer. There are lots of interesting things about this set of methods. One of its joys is that it stimulates research. As the sociologist Larry Griffin (2007) puts it, it asks the analyst 'a series of questions about the causal connections among actions... It relentlessly probes the analyst's construction, comprehension and interpretation of the event.' In other words, it makes you think.

Part Three
Beyond the tests

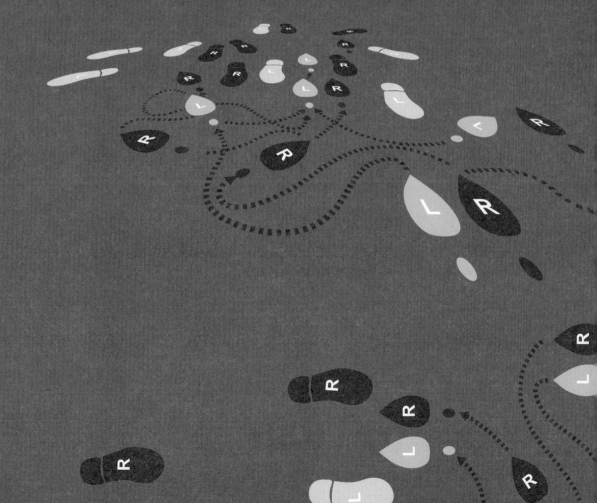

Chapter 12
Exercises

I have departed from the usual textbook practice of placing exercises immediately after each set of tests. Such a practice neither stretches the memory nor reflects the reality of conducting research: you are expected to work out for yourself which tests are appropriate in any given circumstances.

On the other hand, I think it is reasonable to tell you that these questions are based upon the following chapters:

- The analysis of differences
- Qualitative analysis
- Correlations, regression and factor analysis

Some understanding of the introductory chapters is also assumed.

Questions

Question 1
40 members of a focus group were asked to choose between two courses of action, Strategy A and Strategy B. No 'abstaining' was allowed. 26 respondents answered in favour of Strategy A. What test should be used and what is the outcome? Accept a significance level of $p < .05$.

Question 2
Wanting to find if women were more likely to take a different view of a policy than men, ratings of the policy were examined. What method is appropriate?

Question 3

Assuming a proven relationship between scores on an admission test and subsequent pass rates on a course, what method should we use to choose applicants?

Question 4

You are looking at the relationship between gender and management level in an industry. The numbers at each hierarchical level are as follows.

Table 12.1

	Chief execs	Senior team	Middle	First line
Female	6	11	20	30
Male	8	18	16	32

What method should we use? Are there significant differences?

Question 5

Three different tax policies are currently being considered. Each politician has been asked for the policy they are most in favour of. There are three political parties. Of the Red Party, 100 favoured Policy A, 230 favoured Policy B, and 150 favoured Policy C. The Blue Party favoured Policies A, B and C as follows: 600, 400, 100. The Green Party favoured Policy A with 180 votes, with 120 for Policy B, and 100 for C.

What design should be adopted? Are the test results significant?

Question 6

The correlation matrix for a mass of data includes many correlations at .9 What should you do?

Question 7

Is a correlation coefficient of .2 significant?

The answers are on page 204

This double page interleaves between the questions and the answers.

If you help yourself by attempting the exercises, the tree will not have suffered in vain.

The answers are on the next page.

Answers to exercises

Answer 1

This is a dichotomous (yes or no) analysis of differences. Use the binomial test. The 26:14 ratio would be significant if a one-tailed level of significance was adopted. But should we really have preconceptions about whether or not people would be inclined to prefer one strategy to the other? I would argue for the two-tailed level of significance. If we adopt this, then we are unable to consider the result to be significantly different from chance.

Answer 2

Mann–Whitney examines the differences between two different sets of individuals on rating scales. (With great confidence in the calibration of the rating scales, the unpaired t test could be used.)

Answer 3

Linear regression. The individual's admission score would be used to predict his or her likely grade.

Answer 4

Chi square test of association. Not significant.

Answer 5

Table 12.2

	Policy A	Policy B	Policy C
Red Party	100	230	150
Blue Party	600	400	100
Green Party	180	120	100

Chi square. Clearly significant.

Answer 6

Check for collinearity, using the 'statistics' option within the Linear Regression menu. It is likely that some variables are saying the same thing. Examine the content of the items and consider removing items which have over-similar meanings. You do want some similarities but not duplication. After such a cull with a lowering of collinearity, you may consider a type of factor analysis to reduce data further, then going into more in-depth examination of the correlations.

Answer 7

Especially when dealing with large amounts of data, this sort of correlation coefficient can indeed be accompanied by an acceptable p value. More to the point is how useful is an effect size of .04? In some cases, 4% of the variance is important, in others not.

Talking point

I decided not to include questions requiring factorial solutions or survival analysis. Apart from sheer laziness, I thought it likely to confuse matters, as answers to such questions could also draw from tests from earlier chapters. On the other hand, if you have suggestions for exercises which would clearly imply relevant answers, please contact me. I will do my best to reply and if I use your suggestion, will certainly acknowledge it in future editions of the book. Similarly, any suggestions or criticisms relating to other parts of the book would be gratefully received.

Chapter 13
Reporting in applied research

Please note that the recommendations in this particular chapter are for people analysing data in applied settings. People who are preparing reports for a university or professional body should refer to the guidance provided by that body or to books on research methods in the area of interest.

One common problem is how to report basic data, for example, in surveys. Sometimes you will use absolute numbers, at other times averages. Your decision is a value judgement but you should make it clear which you are using, for your own sanity as well as the reader's comprehension. For example, when comparing financial data from different countries, percentages would usually make more sense given the usually different population sizes, but absolute figures would make sense if disparity of size was the very point of the exercise.

When referring to a particular variable, we usually want to represent the mean as the measure of central tendency. However, the median is preferred in the case of skewed data, as it is not sensitive to extremes.

Use a spreadsheet such as Microsoft Excel for charts. These are generally more easily adaptable that the products of statistical packages. Pie charts are particularly useful for comparing data where the data is exclusive, that is, everything falls into one category or another. Columns are commonly used for clear contrasts of data, although bar charts are more suitable in the case of several categories as they allow a chart to stretch down a page with titles of the categories at the side.

You will also find increasingly complex graphs, with one layer sitting on another. If you must use these, be careful to explain what it is that is being portrayed.

I often see these in newspapers and am not always sure what it is that I am looking at.

Spreadsheets can even be used to create simple correlation charts.

In the discussion below, I shall refer to three levels of sophistication of the likely readers of your research. Such a reader may be the commissioner of research, or a line manager within your own organisation or an external body. The sophisticated reader will know as much as you do about the use of statistical methods, and probably more. The intermediate reader is likely to at least remember about significance levels from their own studies in the past. The unsophisticated reader will not necessarily understand the difference between statistical significance and the everyday use of the word; p values will mean nothing.

Written reporting

First, in reporting significant results outside academia, we dispense with the null hypothesis. Although I explained the term while explaining methodology, the lay reader is not concerned with such apparent paradoxes. You merely report that the result is 'significant' or 'not significant'. If your audience is relatively sophisticated, you may put it as being 'significant ($p < .05$)' or 'significant to level $p < .05$'; with an intermediate level of sophistication, the first time such a citation is made, you may explain that this means that the likelihood of the results being a matter of chance are only 5 in a hundred. You would only consider using references to 'two-tailed' or 'one-tailed' hypotheses for sophisticated readers; even for such an audience, a discussion of whether or not the effect was expected in a particular direction would be helpful.

Following on from this point is effect size. The term effect size would only be used with a sophisticated audience. It should be noted that until very recently, the concept (or proportion of variance) has rarely been mentioned in introductory books. The intermediate reader could be told that this is a 'large', 'medium-sized' or 'small' effect; do not bother with r^2 (or other references to the names of actual statistics). Be even more sparing with unsophisticated audiences; mentions of particularly large (or small) effects are sufficient.

Third, only cite the statistical tests used on a regular basis with sophisticated audiences. With the intermediate reader, the occasional mention of Friedman, or whatever, should only be given in parentheses – 'the result was significant to $p < .05$ (Friedman)' just to impress a little. Don't cite at all with the lowest level of reader.

Fourth, unlike in academic research, the reader does *not* want to know how you organised your data (unless this is strictly relevant to your audience). You should still, of course, record your methods so that they can be replicated as necessary. In the case of removing outliers, however, the sophisticated reader may be informed; they are likely to understand the relevance or otherwise of such data.

In general terms, just provide the reader with relevant results, ones which have a bearing on the purpose of the research. It should not resemble an academic thesis, should not be long and, while not an entertainment, should be readable and cogent.

Verbal reporting

As with written reports, your content needs to be limited – only more so! People are usually unable to listen for long to continuous talk. So follow the previous recommendations for content limitation in written reporting, but also consider the following ways of countering information overload and boredom.

A good idea is to show one idea at a time, with a chart and possibly the relevant statistic (bearing in mind the audience), on one page.

If using slide-show presentations, try to keep the information interesting. At the very least, have clauses sliding in from the side. Don't have large slabs of text if you can possibly avoid this.

Avoid the common habit of using patterns and different colours. These can distract the reader and can even make the presentation difficult to read. Good old black and white is very effective. Try to use the same format throughout.

Whereas your written report will include the usual connecting sentences which provide a cogent, flowing narrative, your visual presentation needs to be a series of points, but in a coherent order. They do not have to be strictly grammatical:

- significant difference in dirty sock usage between men and women;
- difficult study conditions;
- small effect size;
- dissimilarity to research on the footwear of Shakespeare's rivals.

You then provide the correct syntax as you read your way down – "There was a significant difference..." – and also connecting comments of interest. "Such an effect size does bring into question how meaningful this particular result will be in the everyday world", "It could be that we are not dealing with comparable phenomenon and that research needs to be carried out on..."

Do prepare the additional comments, at least mentally. Listeners tend to feel rather short-changed when a presenter merely reads sentences off a screen; they think (reasonably) that they can do this by themselves.

In order for this to run smoothly you may find it useful to rehearse your patter once or twice, preferably in front of a sympathetic audience. Do try to address the audience wherever possible and be professional even in rehearsals. This increases the chances of automating your performance. You don't need to learn the words by heart but you do want things to run smoothly. (And if it's your first time, don't worry: everybody else in your audience is likely to have experienced this or knows they have it coming.)

Talking point

Clear categorisation and knowing what to omit are central to good report-writing. Unfortunately, however, there are two ways of considering this point. Making things clearer to the audience is clearly one. Playing to the audience is another: there can be a tension between the audience's needs and objectivity. A maxim in UK research circles (c 2006) suggests that, in many cases, researchers are not helping to develop evidence-based policy so much as producing policy-based evidence! May your ideals go with you....

Chapter 14
A taste of further statistical methods

This book is for beginners, but nevertheless a lot of useful research can be conducted with the methods discussed here. I offer here, however, a taste of what more advanced methods can do. In order not to create confusion, only a few types of test will be considered, building upon what you have already learned. (A possible source of in-depth information is cited at the end of each entry.)

MANOVA – multivariate analysis of variance

This allows the user to examine more than one dependent variable at a time. This can be very useful if the interplay of predictors may have a differential effect on a set of criteria which may or not be clearly related. If, for example, the declared supporters of two or three political parties were measured on ratings of altruism and charity-giving, would they hold significantly different views on both or would the attitude to only one of these measures be different according to political belief? (Huberty and Olejnik, 2006)

Cluster analysis

Viewed from the perspective of a correlation matrix, the columns – the variables – are examined by factor analysis, reducing the number of variables to a smaller set of underlying dimensions. In surveys, for example, you can work out if particular types of attitudes underlie a range of responses.

Cluster analysis is another form of data reduction technique, but here the focus is upon the *rows* of the matrix, which represent cases: observations of phenomena or the individual participants. Here, data is reduced to 'objects' or groups of people. In a range of sales figures, we may discover that particular groups of people – retired or students, maybe – tend towards different purchasing patterns. So, in an inversion of factor analysis, we look not at core constructs but at the behaviour of clusters of individuals or groups of data. (Everitt et al, 2011)

Logistic regression

At times you are going to find that much of your research data consists of zeroes and ones (yes/no). Although categorical (or qualitative) methods have their place, when you have relatively rich data sets including multiple predictors, you are likely to want to use methods which can sensitively weigh up the relative contributions of different variables. Logistic regression has a range of uses and allows the sophisticated measurement of binary data. (Hosmer and Lemeshow, 2000)

Cox's regression (also known as the Cox model)

This variant of survival analysis was mentioned in Chapter 11. It takes into account the effect of several variables on the time until an event. It can give more accurate results than the Kaplan–Meier function, but requires certain assumptions to be met (Walters, 2009).

Talking point

Although other useful tests are available, many researchers rarely operate beyond the statistical foothills. If you mastered all of the techniques in this book, which I hope proved enjoyable and useful to you, this may be all that you need; but having gained such skills, you should be able to benefit from more advanced training as required.

References

Arndt, S., Turvey, C. and Andreasen, N. (1999) 'Correlating and predicting psychiatric symptom ratings: Spearman's r versus Kendall's tau correlation', *Journal of Psychiatric Research*, vol 33, no 2, pp 97–104.

Bland, M. (2000) *An introduction to medical statistics* (3rd edn), Oxford: Oxford University Press.

Brown, T. (2006) *Confirmatory Factor Analysis for Applied Research*, New York: Guilford Press.

Campbell, K. (1989) 'Dangers in using analysis of covariance procedures', paper presented at the annual meeting of the Mid–South Educational Research Association (17th, Louisville, KY, Nov 9–11, 1988), ERIC (Educational Resources Center), www.eric.ed.gov.

Cattell, R. (1966) 'The scree test for the number of factors', *Multivariate Behavioral Research*, vol 1, pp 629–637.

Clark–Carter, D. (1997) *Doing quantitative psychological research: from design to report*, Hove: Psychology Press.

Creswell, J. (2008) *Research design: qualitative, quantitative, and mixed methods approaches*, London: Sage.

Dallal, G. (2001) 'Multiple comparison procedures', www.jerrydallal.com/LHSP/mc.htm.

Davies, M. (2007) *Doing a successful research project: using qualitative or quantitative methods,* Basingstoke, UK: Palgrave Macmillan.

Davis, C. (2010) *Statistical testing in practice with StatsDirect*, Tamarac, FL: Llumina Press.

Day, R. and Quinn, G. (1989) 'Comparisons of treatments after an analysis of variance in ecology', *Ecological Monographs*, vol 59, no 4, pp 433–463.

Embretson, S. and Reise, S. (2000) *Item response theory for psychologists*, Hove: Psychology Press.

Everitt, B., Landau, S., Leese, M. and Stahl, D. (2011) *Cluster Analysis*, Oxford: Wiley-Blackwell.

Field, A. (2009) *Discovering statistics using SPSS*, London: Sage.

Fisher, R. (1935) *The design of experiments*, Edinburgh: Oliver and Boyd.

Furman University (2007) 'SPSS tutorials, lesson 14: analysis of covariance', http://eweb.furman.edu/~lpace/SPSS_Tutorials/lesson14.html.

Games, P. (1971) 'Multiple comparison of means', *American Educational Research Journal*, no 8(3), pp 531–565.

Greene, J. and D'Oliveira, M. (1982). *Learning to use statistical tests in psychology: A student's guide*, Milton Keynes: Open University Press.

Griffin, L. (2007) 'Historical sociology, narrative and event–structure analysis: Fifteen years later', Sociologica, *Italian Journal of Sociology* on line, no 3.

Hess, B. and Olejnik, S. (1997) 'Top ten reasons why most omnibus tests should be abandoned', *Journal of Vocational Education Research*, vol 22, no 4, pp 219–232.

Hilton, A. and Armstrong, R. (2006) 'Stat note 6 : post hoc ANOVA tests', *Microbiologist*, September, http://eprints.aston.ac.uk/9317/1/Statnote_6.pdf.

Hosmer, D. and Lemeshow, S. (2000), *Applied Logistic Regression*, Oxford: Wiley-Blackwell.

Howell, D. (2011) 'Multiple comparisons with repeated measures', www.uvm.edu/~dhowell/StatPages/More_Stuff/RepMeasMultComp/RepMeasMultComp.html.

Huberty, C. and Olejnik, S. (2006) *Applied MANOVA and Discriminant Analysis*, Oxford: Wiley-Blackwell.

Huck, S. (2008) *Statistical misconceptions*, London: Routledge.

IBM (2011) *IBM SPSS Statistics 20 Core System User's Guide.* This and other SPSS manuals are available at: library.uvm.edu/services/statistics/SPSS20Manuals/.

Kahneman, D. (2011) *Thinking, fast and slow*, London: Allen Lane.

Kaiser, H. (1960). 'The application of electronic computers to factor analysis', *Educational and Psychological Measurement*, vol 20, pp 141–151.

Kinnear, P. and Gray, C. (2004) *SPSS 12 made simple*, Hove: Psychology Press.

Klein, J. and Moeschberger, M. (2003) *Survival Analysis: Techniques for Censored and Truncated Data*, New York: Springer.

Kleinbaum, D, Kupper, L, Nizam, A. and Muller, K. (2008) *Applied regression analysis and other multivariable methods*, Pacific Grove, CA: Duxbury Press.

Kline, R. (2010) *Principles and Practice of Structural Equation Modeling*, New York: Guilford Press.

Maughan, S., Styles, B., Lin, Y. and Kirkup, C. (2009) *Partial estimates of reliability: parallel form reliability in the Key Stage 2 science tests*, Slough: National Foundation for Educational Research.

Miles, J. and Shevlin, M. (2000) *Applying regression and correlation: a guide for students and researchers*, London: Sage.

Nelder, J. (1971) 'Discussion', *Journal of the Royal Statistical Society*, series B, no 33, pp 244–246.

Nelder, J. (1999) 'From statistics to statistical science', *Statistician*, no 48, pp 257–267.

Parker, R. (1979) *Introductory statistics for biology*, London: Edward Arnold.

Pearce, S. (1993) 'Data analysis in agricultural experimentation. III. Multiple comparisons', *Experimental Agriculture*, no 29, pp 1–8.

Perrigot, R., Cliquet, G. and Mesbah, M. (2004) 'Possible applications of survival analysis in franchising research', *International Review of Retail, Distribution and Consumer Research*, vol 14, no 1, pp 129–143.

Plackett, R. (1971) *Introduction to the theory of statistics*, Edinburgh: Oliver and Boyd.

Pohlmann, J. (2004) 'Use and interpretation of factor analysis in the Journal of Educational Research: 1992–2002', *The Journal of Educational Research*, vol 98, pp 14–23.

Preece, D. (1982) 'T is for trouble (and textbooks): a critique of some examples of the paired-samples t–test', *The Statistician*, no 31, pp 169–195.

Rice, W. (1989) 'Analysing tables of statistical tests', *Evolution*, no 43, pp 223–225.

Roberts, P., Priest, H. and Traynor, M. (2006) 'Reliability and validity in research', *Nursing Standard*, vol 20, no 44, pp 41–45.

Roscoe, J. (1975) *Fundamental research statistics for the behavioral sciences*, New York: Holt, Rinehart and Winston.

Sato, T. (1996) 'Type 1 and type 2 errors in multiple comparisons', *Journal of Psychology*, vol 130, no 3, pp 293–302.

Sekaran, U. and Bougie, R. (2009) *Research methods for business*, Chichester: John Wiley and Sons.

SSTARS (2011) 'Pairwise comparisons in SAS and SPSS', University of Kentucky, www.uky.edu/ComputingCenter/SSTARS/www/documentation MultiplemComparisons_3.htm.

Temple, J. (1978) 'The use of factor analysis in geology', *Mathematical Geology*, vol 10, no 4, pp 379-387.

Thurstone, L. (1947) *Multiple-factor analysis*, Chicago: University of Chicago Press.

Tsoumakas, G., Lefteris, A. and Vlahavas, I. (2005) 'Selective fusion of heterogeneous classifiers', *Selective Data Analysis*, no 9, pp 511–525.

Walters, S. (2009) 'What is a Cox model?', Newmarket: Hayward Medical Communications, www.whatisseries.co.uk

Wyseure, G. (2003) 'Multiple comparisons', http://www.agr.kuleuven.ac.be/vakken/statisticsbyR/ANOVAbyRr/multiplecomp.htm.

Yerkes, R. and Dodson, J. (1908) 'The relation of strength of stimulus to rapidity of habit-formation', *Journal of Comparative Neurology and Psychology*, vol 18, pp 459–482.

Index of concepts

Index of tests